FUNDAMENTALS OF COUNTERTERRORISM

ASPEN PUBLISHERS

FUNDAMENTALS OF COUNTERTERRORISM

Amos N. Guiora
Professor of Law
S.J. Quinney College of Law
University of Utah

Wolters Kluwer
Law & Business

AUSTIN   BOSTON   CHICAGO   NEW YORK   THE NETHERLANDS

Aspen Publishers
Attn: Permissions Department
76 Ninth Avenue, 7th Floor
New York, NY 10011-5201

To contact Customer Care, e-mail customer.care@aspenpublishers.com, call 1-800-234-1660, fax 1-800-901-9075, or mail correspondence to:

Aspen Publishers
Attn: Order Department
PO Box 990
Frederick, MD 21705

Printed in the United States of America.

1 2 3 4 5 6 7 8 9 0

ISBN 978-0-7355-7163-1

Library of Congress Cataloging-in-Publication Data

Guiora, Amos N., 1957-
   Fundamentals of counterterrorism / Amos N. Guiora.
      p. cm.
   Includes index.
   ISBN 978-0-7355-7163-1
1. Terrorism. 2. Terrorism—Prevention. 3. Terrorism—Government policy.
4. Security, International. 5. National security—Law and legislation.
6. Terrorists. 7. Police questioning. I. Title.

K5256.G83 2008
363.325—dc22

                                                        2008044236

About Wolters Kluwer Law & Business

Wolters Kluwer Law & Business is a leading provider of research information and workflow solutions in key specialty areas. The strengths of the individual brands of Aspen Publishers, CCH, Kluwer Law International and Loislaw are aligned within Wolters Kluwer Law & Business to provide comprehensive, in-depth solutions and expert-authored content for the legal, professional and education markets.

CCH was founded in 1913 and has served more than four generations of business professionals and their clients. The CCH products in the Wolters Kluwer Law & Business group are highly regarded electronic and print resources for legal, securities, antitrust and trade regulation, government contracting, banking, pension, payroll, employment and labor, and healthcare reimbursement and compliance professionals.

Aspen Publishers is a leading information provider for attorneys, business professionals and law students. Written by preeminent authorities, Aspen products offer analytical and practical information in a range of specialty practice areas from securities law and intellectual property to mergers and acquisitions and pension/benefits. Aspen's trusted legal education resources provide professors and students with high-quality, up-to-date and effective resources for successful instruction and study in all areas of the law.

Kluwer Law International supplies the global business community with comprehensive English-language international legal information. Legal practitioners, corporate counsel and business executives around the world rely on the Kluwer Law International journals, loose-leafs, books and electronic products for authoritative information in many areas of international legal practice.

Loislaw is a premier provider of digitized legal content to small law firm practitioners of various specializations. Loislaw provides attorneys with the ability to quickly and efficiently find the necessary legal information they need, when and where they need it, by facilitating access to primary law as well as state-specific law, records, forms and treatises.

Wolters Kluwer Law & Business, a unit of Wolters Kluwer, is headquartered in New York and Riverwoods, Illinois. Wolters Kluwer is a leading multinational publisher and information services company.

To my parents, whose life experiences are an extraordinary tale,

for their unconditional love, support, and dedication

Amos N. Guiora is professor of law at the S.J. Quinney College of Law, University of Utah.

Professor Guiora teaches Criminal Law, Criminal Procedure, International Law, Global Perspectives on Counterterrorism, and Religion and Terrorism. He is also a Research Fellow at the International Institute on Counter-Terrorism, The Interdisciplinary Center, Herzeliya, Israel and has been awarded a Senior Specialist Fulbright Fellowship for The Netherlands in 2008. His classroom teaching incorporates innovative scenario-based instruction to address national and international security issues.

Professor Guiora writes and lectures extensively on issues such as "Legal Aspects of Counterterrorism," "Global Perspectives on Counterterrorism," "Terror Financing," "International Law and Morality in Armed Conflict," "Educating IDF Commanders and Soldiers on International Law and Morality," and "Religion and Terrorism."

He has testified before the U.S. Senate Judiciary Committee, "Improving Detainee Policy: Handling Terrorism Detainees within the American Justice System," (June, 2008) and the U.S. House of Representatives Committee on Homeland Security, Subcommittee on Intelligence, Information Sharing and Terrorism Risk Assessment, "Effectiveness, Accountability and Resilience in Homeland Security," (May, 2008).

In addition to numerous op-eds and journal articles on topics related to counterterrorism, his publications include:

- *Global Perspectives on Counterterrorism, 2007, Aspen Publishers*
- *Constitutional Limits on Coercive Interrogation, 2008, Oxford University Press*
- *Freedom of Religion-Freedom from Religion: Rights, Conflicts and Obligations — A Comparative Perspective: Israel, The Netherlands, Turkey, UK and the US, forthcoming, 2009, Oxford University Press*
- *Editor, Annual Review — Top Ten Global Security Law Review Articles, Oxford University Press*

Professor Guiora has also appeared as an expert commentator for CNN, The Washington Post, PBS, The New York Times, The Los Angeles Times, BBC, C-Span, The Christian Science Monitor, Fox TV, the New York Daily News, KQV Newsradio Pittsburgh, Wisconsin Public Radio, Minnesota Public Radio, NPR, Fox TV, Chicago Sun Times, Voice of America, Wall Street Journal, WCPN, Associated Press, and the Seattle Post-Intelligence.

SUMMARY OF CONTENTS

Contents   *xiii*

Preface   *xix*

INTRODUCTION   1

1 *DEFINING TERRORISM AND
   COUNTERTERRORISM*   7

2 *WHAT MOTIVATES THE TERRORIST?*   29

3 *GEOPOLITICS AND COUNTERTERRORISM*   47

4 *THE LIMITS OF POWER AND OPERATIONAL
   COUNTERTERRORISM*   65

5 *RULES OF ENGAGEMENT*   79

6 *SEPARATION OF POWERS AND CHECKS AND
   BALANCES*   91

7 *INTERROGATION OF TERRORISM SUSPECTS*   105

8 *STATE-SPONSORED TERRORISM*   123

9 *TERRORISM AND THE MEDIA*   137

10 *FRAMING HOMELAND SECURITY*   **151**

11 *GOING FORWARD*   **165**

Index   *175*

CONTENTS

Preface   xix

INTRODUCTION   1

1   *DEFINING TERRORISM AND
     COUNTERTERRORISM*   7

   A. INTRODUCTION   7
   B. DEFINING TERRORISM   7
      1. How Different States Define Terrorism   9
      2. Intimidation   13
      3. Advancement of a Cause   13
   C. PROPOSED DEFINITION OF TERRORISM   14
   D. HOW ARE CAUSES ADVANCED?   17
      1. Terror Financing   18
      2. Terror Bombings   20
   E. DOES TERRORISM NEED TO BE DEFINED?   21
      1. The Commander's Perspective   22
      2. The General's Perspective   22
      3. The International Community's Perspective   23
   F. DEFINING COUNTERTERRORISM   26
      1. Developing a Counterterrorism Strategy   26
      2. Three Models   27
   G. CONCLUSION   28

2   *WHAT MOTIVATES THE TERRORIST?*   29

   A. INTRODUCTION   29

B. DEDICATION   29
C. THE "EXTRA" FACTOR   30
D. TERRORIST MANIFESTOS   34
E. HATRED AND REVENGE   35
F. PSYCHOLOGY   36
G. IDEOLOGY   40
  1. Nationalism/Separatism   40
  2. Religion as Ideology   41
     a. Fundamentalist Movements   42
     b. The Mission   43
     c. Applying Motivations   44

3 GEOPOLITICS AND
   COUNTERTERRORISM   47
A. INTRODUCTION   47
B. IS GLOBAL ISLAMIC TERRORISM A GENUINE
   PHENOMENON?: HAMAS
   AS A CASE STUDY   49
  1. On Whose Behalf Is Hamas Acting?   51
  2. Who Supports Hamas and Why   51
  3. The Relationship Between Religion and Terrorism   52
  4. Geopolitics and the Local Terror
     Group   52
C. GLOBAL ISLAMIC TERRORISM AND
   "AL-QAEDA FRANCHISED"   54
  1. Franchises — Homegrown Terrorism   56
  2. Preventing Homegrown Terrorism   57
D. WHEN LOCAL AND INTERNATIONAL
   TERRORISM MIX   60

4 THE LIMITS OF POWER AND
   OPERATIONAL COUNTERTERRORISM   65
A. INTRODUCTION   65
B. LIMITING COLLATERAL DAMAGE   66
C. HOW TO TREAT TERRORIST SUSPECTS   70
D. THE HYBRID PARADIGM   72
E. HOW DO SOLDIERS KNOW HOW TO ACT?   74

F. THE CONSEQUENCES OF VIOLATING THE
   LIMITS OF POWER   77
G. CONCLUSION   78

5 *RULES OF ENGAGEMENT*   79

A. INTRODUCTION   79
B. INTELLIGENCE INFORMATION   80
C. TARGETED KILLING   81
   1. Target's Behavior   83
   2. Soldier's Conduct and Training   84
   3. Degree of Danger Posed   85
   4. Unit's Previous Conduct/Experience   86
D. ALTERNATIVE MEANS TO NEUTRALIZE
   THE THREAT   87
E. MILITARY NECESSITY AND "OPEN FIRE"
   ORDERS   88
F. CONCLUSION   89

6 *SEPARATION OF POWERS AND CHECKS
       AND BALANCES*   91

A. INTRODUCTION   91
B. HOW—AND WHERE—DO WE STRIKE A
   BALANCE?   92
C. AHARON BARAK'S THEORY OF JUDICIAL
   REVIEW   93
D. THE NECESSITY OF CONGRESSIONAL
   OVERSIGHT   94
   1. The Judiciary   98
   2. The Public   98
   3. The Media   99
   4. Executive Self-Restraint   99
E. CONCLUSION   103

7 *INTERROGATION OF TERRORISM
       SUSPECTS*   105

A. INTRODUCTION   105
B. WHEN MESSAGES ARE MIXED: ABU GHRAIB   106

C. WHAT TECHNIQUES ARE PERMISSIBLE?   107
D. THE LEGAL IMPLICATIONS OF TORTURE: THE
   ADMISSIBILITY OF CONFESSIONS AT TRIAL   110
E. THE LIMITS OF U.S. INTERROGATION POLICY   112
   1. In the Absence of Clarity   112
   2. The Limits of Detention   113
F. WHAT IS TORTURE?   114
G. WHY TORTURE?   117
   1. Interrogators   118
   2. The Public   120
   3. Legal-Judicial Infrastructure   121

8 STATE-SPONSORED TERRORISM   123

A. INTRODUCTION   123
B. INDEPENDENCE   124
C. HOW DO STATES RESPOND TO
   STATE-SPONSORED TERRORISM?   125
   1. The Bush Doctrine   126
   2. Who Are State Sponsors of Terrorism?   128
   3. How to Engage Sponsors, Proxies, and Sponsored
      Terror Groups Effectively   128
D. THE LEGITIMACY OF RESPONDING TO
   SPONSORS AND PROXIES MILITARILY   129
E. LEGITIMACY AND EFFECTIVENESS   133
F. CONCLUSION   135

9 TERRORISM AND THE MEDIA   137

A. INTRODUCTION   137
B. THE MEDIA   138
   1. A New Vision of Media Responsibility?   140
   2. Post-9/11 Coverage   142
C. POLICY MAKERS   143
D. TERRORISTS   144
   1. Core Supporters   145
   2. Potential Recruits   146
   3. Impacted Citizens   147

4. International Opinion   148
E. CONCLUSION   148

10 FRAMING HOMELAND SECURITY   151

A. INTRODUCTION   151
B. EFFECTIVENESS   151
  1. Analyzing the Threat   152
  2. Collateral Damage   154
  3. Civil Liberties   154
  4. Verifying Intelligence   154
  5. Frequency of Reporting   155
  6. Fiscal Responsibility   155
  7. Geopolitical Concerns   155
  8. Rule of Law   156
C. HOMELAND SECURITY   156
  1. Differentiating Homeland Security from Other
    Terms   157
  2. Structuring Homeland Security   158
    a. Prevent and Disrupt Terrorist Attacks 158
    b. Border Control and Immigration   159
    c. Critical Infrastructure   159
D. GLOBAL PERSPECTIVES ON HOMELAND
  SECURITY   161
  1. Israel   161
  2. United Kingdom   162
E. ACCOUNTABILITY   162
F. CONCLUSION   163

11 GOING FORWARD   165

A. INTRODUCTION   165
B. PICKING YOUR BATTLES   166
C. HOW WILL A DECISION BE VIEWED BY
  THE COMMUNITY?   167
D. IS THE INTELLIGENCE SOLID?   168
E. A NEW VISION OF SELF-DEFENSE   168
F. MAKING A DECISION   171
G. CONCLUSION   173

Index   175

PREFACE

The idea for this book was born in May 2007 over lunch with members of the Aspen family: Steve Errick, Carol McGeehan, Rick Mixter, and John Devins. I had flown to Waltham, Massachusetts to discuss various marketing strategies related to my book, *Global Perspectives on Counterterrorism*, and future projects. Someone — I confess to not recall who — suggested I write a book addressing varied and sundry issues seminal to counterterrorism for multiple audiences. Not too lawyerly; not too general; not too specific; suited for undergraduates; adaptable for law students. We all looked at each other. Rick Mixter suggested that I write in such a manner that the chapters could be viewed both as part of the book and also as more modular, stand-alone material to complement a related course or seminar.

The day of the meeting has special meaning for me. In addition to agreeing to write this book, that evening my good friend and fellow Aspen author Craig Nard and his wife, Patty, hosted an absolutely lovely farewell party in their beautiful home for Andy Morriss and me, as we were both leaving Case Western Law School; Andy to Illinois, I to Utah. While the evening was sad, it also represented moving forward to a law school with an exciting, vigorous, innovative Dean, Hiram Chodosh, who welcomed me with open arms and an extraordinary willingness to offer me whatever assistance I required for my new project — this book.

Within a couple of weeks I had two research assistants, one, RuthAnne Frost, for this book, the other, Artemis Vamianakis, for a co-authored piece with my former Dean and good friend, Gerry Korngold. In other words, I truly was moving forward.

This has been a most enjoyable book to write for it enabled me to address numerous issues I have long thought about. For that, I am most grateful to Aspen. As the book began to crystallize in my mind I requested (actually, conditioned) that John Devins be appointed editor. I am truly fortunate to have JD on my side. He is the best.

RuthAnne's contributions have been invaluable—whether editing, researching, arguing, or creating the phenomenal graphics critical to the book, she truly has been a vital member of the team.

I owe many thanks to the reviewers of the first draft—their thoughtful, insightful, and frank comments contributed significantly to the final product. I hope I have done their efforts justice. Needless to say, all faults and errors are mine.

FUNDAMENTALS OF COUNTERTERRORISM

INTRODUCTION

Over the course of twenty years, I have provided legal and policy advice on critical counterterrorism decisions made by Israel Defense Forces (IDF) commanders in the West Bank and Gaza Strip, and have spent long hours with General Security Service interrogators in detention centers in Israel, the West Bank, and the Gaza Strip. In various postings in the Judge Advocate General Corps, I have filed indictments, acquitted or convicted, and recommended the administrative detention of thousands of Palestinians accused of involvement in terrorist activity. Taken together, these years of firsthand experience in the legal, policy, and operational aspects of counterterrorism have afforded me a unique insight into the motivation and worldview of the terrorist, and about the nature of terrorism in general, all of which inform the pages of this book.

Involvement in significant operational counterterrorism decisions enabled me to understand from close up the dilemma of the decision maker. The legal and policy aspects of operational counterterrorism require both an understanding of the relevant law and of operational considerations. A commander must be sensitive to the law; the legal advisor must be sensitive to the pressures "in the field."

Part of my job was to explain to the foreign press the legal and policy aspects of Israel's counterterrorism measures. While the effort was occasionally frustrating, the undeniable result was an enormous respect and sensitivity for perceptions. What the IDF argued was self-defense, journalists perceived as the unnecessary use of force. Explaining to a skeptical press corps issues such as military necessity, proportionality, collateral damage, and alternatives to the use of force was always challenging.

It is impossible to explain all of counterterrorism to all audiences in all of its aspects in a single volume. The more modest goal of this book is to address a number of core issues central to counterterrorism without which it is impossible to begin understanding the more nuanced complexities of the topic. Some will argue that additional issues should have been addressed here; others will question why I have included what I have. To each set of critics I answer: you are both correct, but a book of this nature cannot be all-inclusive.

I have tried to give readers representing different audiences a sampling of issues germane to counterterrorism. Though the legal aspects of counterterrorism are discussed where appropriate, this is not intended to be a law school casebook with exhaustive legal analysis. Because of a growing interest at the undergraduate and graduate level for terrorism-related courses, the book incorporates material intended to reach those students as well. Based on my numerous public speaking engagements, it is also clear that there is enormous interest among the general public for a book of this nature. Thus I have sought to explain counterterrorism in a broadly accessible manner.

I think it important to note that this book is obviously and by necessity a reflection of my twenty years' experience with operational counterterrorism in the IDF. It should be clear, however, that there is no intention whatsoever to suggest that the IDF's decisions are always right. Far from it. Nor do I intend this volume to serve as a paean to the IDF. It is not. But I do agree with the much-stated suggestion that Israel is the world's leading terrorism/counterterrorism laboratory and, as such, offers a rare opportunity to study a topic of such high importance to the modern world.

Regarding the "voice" of the book, I have made a conscious decision, when appropriate, to relate directly events I have been directly involved in or matters known to me personally whose authenticity I can vouch for (though the name of the actual decision maker will not appear for obvious reasons). I believe this approach will better assist the reader in understanding counterterrorism in a less formal, more direct and immediate way. I also believe it is a more effective way to convey the urgency of many critical situations that arise in operational counterterrorism—those situations which do not lend themselves to some of the drier, more detached academic approaches to the subject.

I intend these eleven chapters to provide material enough for a broad foundational study of counterterrorism, while also allowing for their individual use as supplemental materials for other related courses. Any book discussing terrorism and counterterrorism must have at its core a definition of the term. Accordingly, the first chapter devotes substantial space to such a definition. While not all readers will agree with my definition, I suggest that any discussion concerning terrorism that does not substantially address the issue is superficial at best. I welcome reader comments and feedback on this subject. If we cannot agree on a precise definition of terrorism, we must at least agree that the careful and thorough debate and discussion necessary to find one is an imperative.

What motivates individuals to commit acts of terrorism? Theories abound, some predicated on research, others on anecdotal evidence. "Know thy enemy" must be the guiding light for any nation-state in developing operational counterterrorism policy. Without seeking to first understand motivation, operational counterterrorism will be nothing more than a shot in the dark. As to the wide range of proposed motivations, I suggest—based on thousands of discussions with thousands of suspected terrorists—that religion is certainly a primary motivator for modern day terrorists.

Terrorism cannot be viewed as an isolated phenomenon. It is part of a larger conflict. Legal and policy decisions must reflect that reality. It is essential that the reader understand that terrorism cannot be viewed separately from other strategic, political, economic, social, and cultural events. Otherwise its larger significance—for the terrorist, the nation-state, and the general public—will be dangerously minimized.

State power is inherently limited. This is particularly true in the context of civil democratic societies where the state cannot do everything to protect itself and its citizens. What are the limits of power in seeking to counter an unseen enemy? How is operational counterterrorism to be conducted if the state adopts the philosophy of self-imposed restraints? What are the dangers to democracy if the state does not impose restraints on its counterterrorism methods? Will the public accept self-imposed restraints or does it demand unrestrained efforts—even at the cost of "round up the usual suspects" and "guilt by association"? While the answers to these questions are problematic, the discussions they require are critical in seeking to understand counterterrorism.

The rules of engagement in counterterrorism—as distinct from traditional war—is a major issue for commanders, policy makers, and soldiers alike. International law is clear as to when soldiers can open fire in traditional warfare against both other soldiers and innocent civilians. However, because operational counterterrorism requires soldiers to engage civilians—albeit, not necessarily innocent civilians, when and against whom a soldier can open fire requires definitions that differ from traditional warfare. The single most important challenge facing a soldier in the context of operational counterterrorism is distinguishing between a civilian who is a legitimate target and one who is not. The challenge with respect to the rules of engagement is articulating—clearly, concisely, and precisely—when an "open fire" order can be given in non-traditional conflict situations.

Democracies, to be vibrant, require Congressional oversight and active judicial review. The executive is charged with protecting the public. It is precisely when democracies are under attack, or perceived attack, that the executive must be restrained, for that is when the chances for excess are the greatest. Justice Jackson's warning in *Korematsu* regarding an "unfettered executive" clearly resonates in the post-9/11 world and is highly applicable to counterterrorism. Understanding counterterrorism requires an analysis of the respective roles of both the legislature and the court regarding separation of powers and checks and balances.

Interrogation is crucial to operational counterterrorism, for without up-to-date, reliable, valid, and viable intelligence counterterrorism is groping in the dark. However, there are clear limits regarding interrogation methods. Torture is illegal (and immoral) and does not lead to actionable intelligence. Nevertheless, the state must gather information both to prevent acts of terrorism and to punish those involved in terrorism. To that extent, I propose an interrogation model that goes beyond the traditional criminal law regime in those cases where interrogation measures are necessary. Understanding counterterrorism requires articulating the limits of interrogation while simultaneously providing interrogators the tools and means necessary to protect the nation-state.

State-sponsored terrorism raises an important question regarding the role of a nation-state in sponsoring terrorism and whether the state targeted by acts of terrorism can respond against the sponsoring state. In the traditional nation-state military relationship, states are engaged in conflict with other states. But terrorism is the conflict between nation-states and non-state entities. The introduction of state sponsors of terrorism adds an additional component. Conflicts exist not only between state and non-state entities but also potentially between two nation-states — one advancing the non-state entity and the other in response to this support. The issue raises important international law questions that go beyond the traditional nation-state relationship.

Terrorism and counterterrorism cannot be understood without examining their relationship with the media. I (and others) suggest that the Munich Olympics massacre of September 1972 represents the beginning of modern-day terrorism. Perhaps no other act of terrorism has been subjected to such intense media scrutiny as the attack on the Israeli athletes by the Palestine Liberation Organization. When ABC's Jim McKay somberly announced "they're all gone," the entire world (literally and figuratively) was watching. There is little doubt that terrorist organizations worldwide quickly came to understand and appreciate television's power in furthering their cause. Decision and policy makers are faced with constant dilemmas in determining how much information to release to the public whether it be intelligence suggesting a *potential* terrorist attack, or information released in the course of an actual attack. This decision-making process has been immeasurably accelerated by the introduction of the Internet and blogs. Counterterrorism decision-making is directly affected by how events are "spun" and presented in the media.

Homeland security requires cooperation among a broad range of government organizations. The United States' efforts to implement homeland security policy provide a useful case study for any democratic state. Nation-states must hold several things in balance: the dangers of collateral damage and reduced civil liberties, accountability to the legislative branch, fiscal responsibility, geopolitical concerns, and the rule of law. Like elsewhere throughout the book, defining terms is essential. Without clearly defining effectiveness and accountability in the context of homeland security, it is all but impossible to develop and implement successful policies.

The final chapter discusses the future of counterterrorism. My fundamental premise with respect to terrorism is that not only is it *undefeatable* — at best terrorism is manageable or minimizable — but that it also represents the new Hundred Years' War. How nation-states respond to the reality of a constant threat will play a role in defining liberal democratic societies for decades to come. States seeking to manage terrorism must clearly articulate goals and come to terms with the inherent limits of counterterrorism. Decision and policy makers must work in tandem with commanders making on-the-ground decisions, and the judicial and legislative branches must exercise their constitutionally mandated role of checking executive power. By learning from the lessons of past failures and successes, democratic nation-states have an opportunity — and the capacity — to minimize error and implement effective operational counterterrorism measures.

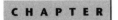

CHAPTER 1

DEFINING TERRORISM AND COUNTERTERRORISM

A. INTRODUCTION

In seeking to understand terrorism and counterterrorism, one of the most controversial and complex issues in an already complex field of study is their respective definitions. Any discussion about terrorism is inherently politicized, thus complicating dispassionate debate. "Terrorism" suggests different meanings depending on the particular social, cultural, political, economic, and military setting. While many use the term, most do not engage in the critical first step of actually defining it.

A great hindrance to a cogent discussion of terrorism has been that the term itself lacks a clear and universal definition. Without precise definitions, any terrorism-related discussion will inevitably be vague and amorphous. This results in ineffective counterterrorism strategies largely devoid of restraints and clearly articulated goals.

B. DEFINING TERRORISM

The definition of terrorism is much debated and discussed. Alex Schmid and Albert Jongman attempted to identify a single, uniform definition in their seminal work, *Political Terrorism: A New Guide to Actors, Authors, Concepts, Data Bases, Theories and Literature.* Schmid and Jongman identified 109 different definitions, which they combined in an effort to create one consensus definition:

> Terrorism is an anxiety-inspiring method of repeated violent action, employed by (semi-) clandestine individual, group or state actors, for

idiosyncratic, criminal or political reasons, whereby — in contrast to assassination — the direct targets of violence are not the main targets. The immediate human victims of violence are generally chosen randomly (targets of opportunity) or selectively (representative or symbolic targets) from a target population, and serve as message generators. Threat- and violence-based communication processes between terrorist (organization), (imperiled) victims and main targets are used to manipulate the main target (audience(s)), turning it into a target of terror, a target of demands or a target of attention, depending on whether intimidation, coercion or propaganda is primarily sought.[1]

It is important to emphasize that terrorism is not a new phenomenon. Societies have confronted what is referred to as terrorism for the past 2,000 years. Part of this may be explained by the simple fact that in many cases, terrorism works.

There is an adage that "one man's terrorist is another man's freedom fighter." This oft repeated phrase makes for an appealing twenty-second sound bite. It does not, however, contribute to the debate in any real way. It does not frame the issue, nor does it provide practical guidance to scholars, students, policy and decision makers, or the general public. A more nuanced approach has been offered by Bruce Hoffman in his acclaimed book, *Inside Terrorism*:

> On one point, at least, everyone agrees: terrorism is a pejorative term. It is a word with intrinsically negative connotations that is generally applied to one's enemies and opponents, or to those with whom one disagrees and would otherwise prefer to ignore.... Hence the decision to call someone or label some organization "terrorist" becomes almost unavoidably subjective, depending largely on whether one sympathizes with or opposes the person/group/cause concerned. If one identifies with the victim of the violence, for example, then the act is terrorism. If, however, one identifies with the perpetrator, the violent act is regarded in a more sympathetic, if not positive (or, at the worst, an ambivalent) light; and it is not terrorism."[2]

One important reason to define terrorism is to ensure that legitimate targets be distinguished from innocent civilians. If a broad definition is adopted, it is paramount that it be cautiously applied.

---

1. Alex P. Schmid & Albert J. Jongman, Political Terrorism: A New Guide to Actors, Authors, Concepts, Data Bases, Theories, and Literature 28 (North-Holland, Amsterdam, 1988).
2. Bruce Hoffman, Inside Terrorism 31 (2006).

1. How Different States Define Terrorism

While different societies face distinct threats predicated on dissimilar political, social, and religious paradigms and regimes, the importance of a global perspective on terrorism cannot be overstated. Examining how different nations define terrorism requires analyzing how legitimate civil rights are balanced with equally legitimate national security considerations. Balancing the two is the essence of how civil democratic societies conduct lawful and moral operational counterterrorism. Otherwise, the state will be sliding down the slippery slope of human and civil rights violations which results in ineffective counterterrorism.

To contribute to effective counterterrorism, the definition of terrorism must enable the state to target individuals who present a threat to the safety of the nations' citizens. Operational measures, however, must reflect tactical and security considerations that ensure the nation-state's subservience to the rule of law.

Figure 1.1 demonstrates how different nations define terrorism. The lack of both uniformity and approach with respect to the definition of terrorism highlights how difficult it is for the international community to present a united front in response to terrorism.

FIGURE 1.1 Global Survey: How Different Nations Define Terrorism

Australia
- Austalian Criminal Code Act 1995, as amended, defines a terrorist act as action that "causes serious physical harm or death to a person, or endangers a person's life or involves serious risk to public health or safety, serious damage to property or serious interference with essential electronic systems; and the action is done or threat is made with the intention of advancing a political, religious or ideological cause and to coerce or influence by intimidation an Australian or foreign government or intimidate the public or section of the public."

Source: "Counter-Terrorism Legislation and Practice: A Survey of Selected Countries," http://image.guardian.co.uk/sys-files/Politics/documents/2005/10/12/foreignterrorlaw1.pdf.

China
- Chinese President Jiang Zemin has said, "Terrorism should be cracked down upon, whenever and wherever it occurs, whoever organizes it, whoever is targeted and whatever forms it takes." According to Human Rights Watch, China has sought to blur the distinctions in order to enlist international

continued on next page

cooperation for its own campaign to eliminate "separatist" efforts by Fulong Gong and Uigar Separatists.

Sources: http://jamestown.org/china_brief/article.php?articleid=2372998; http://hrw.org/un/chr59/counter-terrorism-bck4htm#P183_32636; and Lam, Willy Wo-Lap, "Widening the Definition of Terrorism," 1 China Brief 8, The Jamestown Foundation (October 25, 2001), available at http://www.jamestown.org/print_friendly.php?volume_id=17&issue_id=636 &article_id=4582.

Germany

- Germany has no legal definition of terrorism, but certain activities (conspiracy, causing explosions, etc.) are covered by separate laws. In the 1970s, membership in a domestic terrorist organization was made illegal under Article 129(a) of the Criminal Code. The ban was later extended to membership of/support for a foreign terrorist organization. In January 2002, the Law on Fighting Terrorism came into force not as a single piece of legislation, but rather as several amendments to previous statutes.

Japan

- "Japan has enacted legislation to address specific terrorist threats rather than a uniform act to counter terrorism.... Under Criminal Code of 1907, crimes such as insurrection, homicide, assault, kidnapping, destruction of property, and rioting can be prosecuted as acts of terrorism.... Although the Code is applicable to the basic common crimes inherent in terrorism, Japan has found it necessary to enact additional legislation to enhance its terrorism counteraction policy."

Source: James, Matthew H., "Keeping the Peace—British, Israeli, and Japanese Legislative Responses to Terrorism."

India

- 2001 antiterrorism ordinance: "Acts done by using weapons and explosive substances or other methods in a manner as to cause or likely to cause death or injuries to any person or persons or loss or damage to property or disruption of essential supplies and services with intent to threaten the unity and integrity of [the state] or to strike terror in any section of the people." In 2003, the Supreme Court of India adopted Schmid's working definition of terrorism, defining acts of terrorism as "peacetime equivalents of war crimes."

Sources: "India Promulgates New Anti-Terrorism Ordinance," Press Trust of India (October 25, 2001) and Madan Singh vs. State of Bihar.

Israel

- Does not define terrorism but describes a terrorist organization as "a body of persons resorting in its activities to acts of violence calculated to cause death or injury to a person or to threats of such acts of violence." (Prevention of Terrorism Ordinance, 1948, 1 L.S.I. 76, (1948), §1.)

continued on next page

Russia

- Russia forbids certain actions through its criminal code. For example, it forbids membership in certain organizations or distributing anti-constitutional propaganda. Russia has been conducting a counterterrorism operation in Chechnya since 1999. In Feb. 2002, Russia's Defense Minister accused Russian allies of "double standards" for failing to condemn Moscow's Chechen enemies as "terrorists" with the same vigor as they pursued Osama bin Laden.

  Source: http://www.tribuneindia.com/2002/20020204/main3.htm.

Spain

- Spain does not have specific antiterrorism laws, and generally approaches terrorism by treating it as an aggravated form of crime. Terrorism-related offenses are set out in the Penal Code and different procedural provisions. The Penal Code states that an act qualifies as a terrorist offense when the purpose of the act is to subvert the constitutional order or to effect serious disturbances of the public order. After the 2004 attacks in Madrid, legislative changes applied mostly to the use and transportation of explosives.

United Kingdom

- "The use of violence for political ends and includes any use of violence for the purpose of putting the public or any section of the public in fear." In the Terrorism Act of 2000, the UK moved away from a Northern Ireland focus and included "religious fundamentalists" and "individuals with fanatical leanings" in their definition.

  Source: Thomas, Philip A., "9/11: USA and UK," Prevention of Terrorism (Temporary Provisions) Act 1989, §20(1) (Eng.).

United States

- Title 22/State Department: Premeditated, politically motivated violence perpetrated against noncombatant targets by subnational groups or clandestine agents, usually intended to influence and audience.
- FBI: unlawful use of force or violence against persons or property to intimidate or coerce a Government, the civilian population, or any segment thereof, in furtherance of political or social objectives.
- Department of Defense: the unlawful use of—or threatened use of—force or violence against individuals or property to coerce or intimidate governments or societies, often to achieve political, religious or ideological objectives.

QUESTIONS TO CONSIDER

1. How much damage does an act have to cause for it to be deemed terrorism?
2. How many people need be involved in the act — both as victims and as perpetrators — for it to be deemed terrorism?
3. What motivations define an act as terrorism?
4. Is there a difference between internal and external threats to the state/society for the threat to be deemed terrorism?
5. Who is a terrorist — the shooter, the driver, the financier, the person providing logistical support, the passive supporter?
6. Who should define terrorism, the state or the actor?
7. What danger does the act have to present to the state for it to be deemed terrorism?
8. Does the state need to be merely endangered for the act to be deemed terrorism?
9. If an act is directed toward a corporation, is it terrorism?
10. Are there limits to the forms of what is referred to as terrorism — ecoterrorism, bioterrorism, nuclearterrorism, cyberterrorism, etc.?
11. Is all terrorism violent?
12. Assuming that not all forms of terrorism are violent, what is the difference between legitimate civil disobedience and non-violent terrorism?
13. If an organization is otherwise prevented from expressing its opposition to a political regime, is terrorism understandable, if not legitimate?
14. If terrorism is an inherently negative word, then does the act of defining terrorism itself suggest judgment of the victor?
15. What is the significance of not defining the term, either deliberately or by default?
16. Does the executive "benefit" from a particular definition of terrorism in the context of executive privilege?
17. What and where is the line between mere crime and terrorism?
18. What is the significance of state-supported terrorism?
19. If terrorism is not defined, is counterterrorism guaranteed to be overbroad?
20. Should terrorism be defined in context of its regional or global considerations?

2. Intimidation

One of the fundamental elements of terrorism concerns non-physical actions by a particular group intended to *intimidate* the civilian population to act, or not act, in a particular manner. Non-physical acts — or what seem to be non-physical — is the initial focus of our examination.

Black's Law Dictionary defines intimidation as "harm inflicted by the use of unlawful threats whereby the lawful liberty of others to do as they please is interfered with. This wrong is of two distinct kinds, for the liberty of action so interfered with may be either that of the plaintiff himself, or that of other persons with resulting damage to the plaintiff."

Terrorism is often associated with physical acts of violence. However, an appropriate definition of terrorism needs to include the element of intimidation, which does not necessarily involve contact, but can be considered terrorism, even though the innocent civilian was not physically harmed.

Intimidation for intimidation's sake is not terrorism. It is more akin to bullying, or the conduct associated with street gangs. Terrorism-based intimidation is action seeking to intimidate the population and influence how the civilian population conducts its daily life.

There are two types of intimidation: direct and indirect. If, as a result of a particular terrorist attack, parents forbid their children from attending an unrelated sporting event held shortly after the attack, the population is reacting out of fear of an additional attack. This is indirect intimidation. While the sporting event was not related to the initial attack, the attack resulted in generalized fear among the civilian population.

In contrast, direct intimidation occurs when the terrorist group sends a specific message to the population. For example, a terrorist group announces that if the government does not undertake action X, the nation's buses will be bombed. If parents then forbid their normally bus-traveling children from riding buses, the parents are victims of direct intimidation.

3. Advancement of a Cause

It is important to consider the difference between criminals and terrorists as we construct a concise definition of terrorism. Terrorists have specific motives distinguishable from criminals. Terrorism is also fundamentally distinguishable from nihilism, which promotes only anarchy, if anything. Terrorists have specific, positive (from their perspective) goals intended to advance their cause.

Nor is terrorism warfare, at least not in the traditional sense. Terrorists do not wear uniforms, fight on behalf of a recognized state, or follow the laws of war (including the international law obligation to limit collateral damage). Therefore, captured terrorists are not prisoners of war because they are not fighting a war.

So what, then, is the motive of those who seek to intimidate? Terrorism involves acting on behalf of something, rather than action merely for the sake of action. The cause is what the movement seeks to advance. Therefore, we must ask whether the specific cause can be advanced through the existing political order using means, such as the legislature, media, public opinion and elections, rather than terrorism? Why are extreme measures required?

Are terrorists frustrated social activists who have come to the realization that their cause can only be advanced through violence directed at innocent civilians as a way to influence the government? Is the essence of terrorism to bring change through means that are inherently illegal?

C. PROPOSED DEFINITION OF TERRORISM

These questions and many more are critical to the debate regarding what constitutes terrorism. Based on an extensive examination of historical and current evidence, I suggest the following definition:

> Terrorism is the killing, injuring, or intimidation of, or causing property damage to, innocent civilians by an individual or group seeking to advance a social, political, economic, or religious cause.

This definition has two elements: the first is the *act* ("the killing, injuring of or causing property damage to innocent civilians ... also to intimidate the innocent civilian population") and the second is the *motive* ("seeking to advance a cause").

What differentiates terrorism from all other motivations is the dedication to a cause devoid of financial inducements. For many committed criminals, the crime is generally related to money, either directly or indirectly. Crimes of passion are the notable exception, as they are clearly distinguishable from a crime committed on behalf of one of the causes listed above or for purposes of financial gain. With respect to crimes related to financial gain, the common criminal will commit a wide array of crimes.

Individuals or groups acting on behalf of a cause — social, political, religious, economic — are acting to advance an "ideal" that benefits a group, rather than the individual. The cause, and how the group benefits from its advancement, is what separate terrorists from criminals. The chart below depicts causes terrorists have sought to advance.

CAUSE	DEFINITION	EXAMPLES
Nationalist/ Liberation	Liberation of a people based on ethnicity, culture or history.	PLO and Hamas fighting for Palestinian independence; the IRA seeking to free Northern Ireland of British presence; Chechen rebels fighting for Chechnya's independence.
Religious	Religious belief predicated by an extreme understanding of duty and obligation to God.	Islamic fundamentalist terrorist groups (some overlap with nationalist/ liberation motives); Christian extremists who bomb abortion clinics; Yigal Amir, an Orthodox Jew who assassinated Israeli Prime Minister Yitzhak Rabin because he opposed the signing of the Oslo Accords.
Ideology	The cause is premised on secular (i.e., unrelated to religion) ideas and beliefs.	Right-wing groups such as white-supremacists in the United States; left-wing groups such as the Red Army in Japan; "eco-terrorist" groups such as Animal Liberation Front and Earth Liberation Front.
State terrorism	State actors who conduct terrorist acts against their own civilian populations for the purpose of maintaining power and control.	Robespierre's "Reign of Terror" during the French Revolution; Francisco Franco's regime in Spain; Nazi Germany.

In analyzing causes in the terrorist context, the relevant question is to what extent will an individual go to further a particular movement? Regardless of the cause, the actions of an individual must be viewed on a spectrum ranging from passive support to active involvement. Figure 1.2 illustrates this spectrum.

FIGURE 1.2   **Levels of Support for Terrorism**

Ideological Support
The individual supports the cause, but not the means by which individuals and organizations are seeking to effectuate goals.
Example: One who supported the re-unification of Northern Ireland with Ireland, but does not support organizations such as the Provisional Irish Republican Army, which participates in illegal acts.

Passive Support
The individual supports the cause as well as the means utilized, but does not participate in the acts themselves.
Example: A 2002 poll conducted by the Jerusalem Media and Communications Centre showed that nearly seven out of 10 Palestinians supported suicide bombings, with about 60 percent expressing "strong" support.[3] These individuals, while not participating in suicide bombings themselves, are offering the bombers their passive support.

Non-Cooperation in Counterterrorism Efforts
The individual supports both the cause and the means utilized, and though not participating in acts themselves, obstructs counterterrorism efforts.

Material Support
The individual is providing terrorists and terrorist organizations materials necessary to conduct terrorist acts, though not participating in the acts themselves. The USA PATRIOT Act defined material support as "any property, tangible or intangible ... or service" offered to a terrorist organization, with exceptions for medicine and religious materials. In testimony before the House Judiciary Committee, the ACLU argued that this definition was overbroad.

Active Support
The individual is directly participating in terrorist acts.

Since the concept of advancing a specific cause is so integral to this book's proposed definition of terrorism, an individual such as Theodore Kaczynski (the "Unabomber") is beyond the scope of our examination. Kaczynski's cause can be described as amorphous at best rather than meeting one of the four specific causes previously identified.

---

3. Martin Asser, Palestinian Support for Suicide Bombers, BBC News (June 28, 2002), http://news.bbc.co.uk/1/low/world/middle_east/2072851.stm/.

However, that is not to dismiss the lone individual acting on behalf of a cause that stands to benefit from that person's conduct. To wit: In July 1989, a Palestinian commandeered a bus on the Tel Aviv–Jerusalem highway, killing 14 passengers and injuring 27 more.

Though nô Arab terrorist organization claimed responsibility for Abd al-Hadi Ghanayem's attack, PLO spokesman Bassam Abu Sharif publicly defended it. In his remand hearing in the Jerusalem District Court, Abd al-Hadi Ghanayem stated that though acting alone, his intention was to contribute to the Palestinian cause. After the attack, shrines were erected both at the site of the bus crash honoring the victims, as well as at the site of Ghanayem's demolished house,[4] supporting his act and the Palestinian cause.

D. HOW ARE CAUSES ADVANCED?

There are many different methods by which terrorist groups seek to advance its cause. These methods represent a typology by which terrorist acts may be categorized. Under the following proposed classification system, the particular terrorist act is categorized according to the act committed.

METHOD	DEFINITION	EXAMPLES (RESULT)
Bioterrorism	The deliberate release of biological agents (bacteria or viruses) capable of producing grave diseases and death. These biological agents are sometimes in their natural form, but more often selectively or genetically altered. These agents can target not only human populations, but also water, food, livestock, crops, etc.	Small pox, pneumonic plague, botulism, tularemia, anthrax

---

4. For thirty years the Israel Defense Forces (IDF) implemented a house demolition policy whereby homes of terror suspects were demolished in an effort to deter others in the terrorist's community from committing similar acts. The legal basis for the act is Article 119 of the Defense Emergency Regulations Act (1945).

CAUSE	DEFINITION	EXAMPLES
Chemical terrorism	The deliberate release of chemical agents capable of producing grave diseases and death.	Chlorine, phosgene, mustard gas, tabun, sarin, soman, hydrogen cyanide and other hemotoxins (chemicals that attack the blood), heavy metal compounds (arsenic, lead, mercury)
Cyberterrorism	The unlawful attack or threat of attack against computer networks and the information stored in them with the intent to intimidate or coerce.[5]	The FBI also defines cybterterrorism as "premeditated, politically motivated attack against information, computer systems, computer programs, and data which results in violence against non-combatant targets by sub-national groups or clandestine agents."
Terror bombing	Any bombing designed to target a civilian population or civilian property.	Suicide bombing, remote-controlled bombings, nuclear

To illustrate the practical application of how a terrorist organization might attempt to advance its cause, two different forms of terrorism are analyzed below. One is terror financing, which as a conduit indirectly contributes to the loss of life. The other is terror bombing, which by its very nature seeks to kill as *many innocent individuals as possible.*

1. Terror Financing

Although certain acts of terrorism, such as the assassination of a political leader, are person (victim) specific in nature, the overwhelming majority are clearly indiscriminate. This is particularly true regarding terror bombings, which will be discussed in the following section. The damage non-violent terrorism exacts can be exceptionally harmful. The obvious reference is to cyberterrorism, which while not directly causing violence as traditionally understood, poses enormously significant and complex dangers in this computer-dependent information age. As illustrated by

---

5. DAN VERTON, BLACK ICE: THE INVISIBLE THREAT OF CYBERTERRORISM (McGraw-Hill, 2003).

the following example, the sophistication level of cyberterrorists (in this case, a money launderer) is extraordinary.

EXAMPLE

A senior vice-president of a major American bank with whom I privately met told the following story: In tracking the movement of money within various accounts, the bank noticed that a number of accounts were particularly active, both in regard to the amount of movement and the monetary figures in question. The senior VP decided he would like to personally meet the individuals as part of the bank's outreach to new, particularly active clients.

In organizing the meeting, the VP came upon a startling discovery — the accounts belonged to a single individual who had developed an astounding 416 AKAs ("also known as") for the purpose, as it was subsequently learned, of financing terrorism.

In response to this development, the bank introduced sophisticated control systems that perhaps should have been in place previously, but were not.

Is this terrorism? Is this "property damage"? Is this "violence"?

As money is the engine that "enables" terrorism, individuals knowingly engaged in financing terrorism meet the terrorist definition. The operative word is "knowingly." In the aftermath of 9/11, the FBI proposed that numerous Islamic charities were fronts for terrorist activity. Individuals who contributed money to those charities argued that they were unaware either of any illegal activity or purpose pertaining to the charities. Because the proposed definition for terrorism presumes deliberate action, acting knowingly is a prerequisite.

Ascertaining the mental state of the individual who donates money to a terrorist organization through an Islamic charity acting as a "front" is difficult. Similarly, determining at what point an individual's mental state correlates to real or material support present significant challenges. The chart below proposes how to consider the donor's actions:

Ignorance	Recklessness	Willful Blindness	Knowledge
Contributes to charity, unaware that charity is a front for terror financing	Individual is unaware that money is going to finance terrorism, but should be aware	Contributes while intentionally avoiding discovering the true nature of the charity	Contributes money, knowing that it will be used to finance terrorism

It is important to note that while the motivation to commit financial-related crimes is financial gain, the motivation behind terrorist financing is ideological rather than profit oriented. This motivational distinction clearly squares with the fundamental difference between common criminals and terrorists.

2. Terror Bombings

Terror bombing is defined within the broadest possible parameters to include the following: dirty bombs, suicide bombings, remote-controlled bombings (without a terrorist exploding himself as differentiated from the suicide bomber), and nuclear weapons. Terror bombing, in the widest possible meaning of the term, is the greatest threat presently posed by terrorists.

Regardless of whether one calls oneself a freedom fighter or terrorist, any bombing that targets innocent civilians is a terrorist bombing. According to former U.S. Senator Henry Jackson,

> The idea that one person's "terrorist" is another's "freedom fighter" cannot be sanctioned. Freedom fighters or revolutionaries don't blow up buses containing non-combatants; terrorist murderers do. Freedom fighters don't set out to capture and slaughter schoolchildren; terrorist murderers do.... It is a disgrace that democracies would allow the treasured word "freedom" to be associated with acts of terrorists.[6]

The targeting of *innocent civilians* in a struggle for independence, or any other struggle for that matter, is not and cannot be condoned by international law. At a minimum, terrorist bombings violate the principles of discrimination and proportionality as articulated by the humanitarian law of armed conflict.[7] Terrorist bombings fail to "draw a firm line of demarcation between civilians and civilian objects, on the one hand, and combatants and military objectives, on the other."[8]

Civilians and civilian targets cannot be the target of an attack. "One of the cardinal principles of humanitarian law of armed conflict is the protection of civilians and civilian objects."[9] Terrorist bombings, by their nature, fail to adhere to this cardinal principle.

---

6. Quoted by George P. Shultz, "The Challenge to Democracies," in Terrorism: How the West Can Win 16, 18 (Benjamin Netanyahu ed., 1986).

7. *See generally* M. Cherif Bassiouni, A Manual on International Humanitarian Law and Arms Control Agreements 31-36 (Transnational Publishers, 2000).

8. *Id.* at 31 (quoting H. Leview, II, The Code of International Armed Conflict 81 (1986)).

9. M. Cherif Bassiouni, A Manual on International Humanitarian Law and Arms Control Agreements 33 (Transnational Publishers, 2000).

Terror bombing is a concern precisely because of its indiscriminate nature. Furthermore, it warrants attention due to its increasingly widespread use, relative ease of production, and difficulty in identifying the perpetrator and preventing its actual detonation. The terror bombing threat clearly differs from other forms of terrorist attacks.

To highlight this uniqueness, one may compare terror bombings to airplane hijackings. Airports already benefit from a security infrastructure. Although the efficacy of these systems is debatable, airport authorities can modify existing resources and procedures to prevent attacks. In the airline industry, the intelligence community can use the records of flight plans to assesses and prioritize risks. There are a finite number of flights to an identifiable number of potential targets (cities). Furthermore, passengers knowingly accept the risk when they choose to fly. Should a passenger prefer, he or she could use another form of transportation.

Terror bombings, on the other hand, by their very nature do not target one specific geographical area or industry. That is the inherent randomness of terror bombings—from a prevention perspective, there are literally an endless number of targets that terrorist organizations deem legitimate.

Any building, bridge, landmark or gathering place is vulnerable. Intelligence gathering capabilities with respect to countering terrorist bombings is exponentially more difficult than in regard to other terrorist tactics. There is no security system to protect all sites, and it is impossible to create one. There are an unlimited number of potential targets and terrorist actors. Prioritizing and subsequently operationalizing counterterrorism with respect to preventing terror bombing presents extraordinary challenges to security forces who must—literally—protect an endless number of potential targets.

Terror bombing is the clearest manifestation of violent terrorism. It presents the most complicated challenge to commanders and policy makers alike. Furthermore, precisely because of its inherent indiscriminate nature, it has the greatest direct effect on the civilian population.

E. DOES TERRORISM NEED TO BE DEFINED?

An additional issue that, while begging to be answered, is seldom addressed: *Does terrorism even need to be defined?* Once again, the answer to this question depends on one's perspective. For example, military commanders may argue that by leaving terrorism undefined, they have greater operational freedom regarding potential targets.

Civil democratic society seeks to balance the legitimate rights of the individual with the equally legitimate national security requirements of the state. That is, in conducting operational counterterrorism (i.e., engaging an individual suspected of involvement in terrorism), the state must balance powerful competing interests. Otherwise violations both of international law (unjustifiable and disproportional collateral damage) and morality (ethical violations) in armed conflict will occur. However, national leaders also have the supreme responsibility of protecting the public. To facilitate discussion, whether terrorism should be defined is analyzed from three different perspectives.

1. The Commander's Perspective

In the Introduction, I suggested that if terrorism is not defined then, commanders—those mandated with determining "in the field" who presents a threat to the state *at that moment* and therefore are subject to "open fire" orders—are afforded greater discretion and flexibility with respect to operational decisions.

Greater operational flexibility would be the direct result of not narrowly defining how and when an individual is threatening national security. The result of not defining terrorism is that the critical factor—determining when an individual is threatening national security—is not institutionalized or codified (by law) but rather would be highly discretionary and subject to enormous personal perspective (the commander). While *perhaps* preferable from the commander's perspective, the question is whether overly broad, unguided discretion serves society's larger purposes.

2. The General Public's Perspective

The general public may favor a "no holds barred" policy in the aftermath of a terrorist attack. President Bush's "bring 'em on" response immediately following 9/11 is a prime example of such a sentiment. An ABC News/*Washington Post* poll conducted in October 2001 found that 92 percent of Americans approved of how the President was conducting the U.S. campaign against terrorism.[10] However, with all due respect to public opinion and emotional responses in the aftermath of an attack, the operational reality and responsibility are very different.

In countless operational planning meetings with IDF commanders that I participated in, the refrain was consistently similar: clearly articulated rules defining legitimate targets are critical to the commander.

---

10. Polling Report.com, "War on Terrorism" *available at* http://www.pollingreport.com/terror.htm/.

While the public—and policy makers—may favor "loose rules" (or perhaps no rules) the commander who bears ultimate responsibility for the conduct of his forces absolutely requires clearly stated rules defining *both* who is a legitimate target and the rules of engagement.

A policy enabling the commander to engage *any* individual suspected of terrorism may satisfy the public's thirst for revenge in the aftermath of an attack. It will, however, potentially lead to criminal sanctions against the commander and his soldiers.

3. The International Community's Perspective

The international community—generally cautious with respect to the use of force—would recoil at an operational paradigm that does not impose limitations on commanders. The objection would be both in terms of international law (conventions and customary), morality in armed conflict, and geopolitical considerations (to be discussed in Chapter 3).

Academics and policy makers have differing viewpoints on the importance of defining terrorism. Presenting the discussion from a "yes-no-maybe" perspective suggests the following in Figure 1.3:

FIGURE 1.3 "Yes-No-Maybe" Perspectives

Yes
- **Boaz Ganor:**[11] "In the struggle against terrorism, the problem of definition is a crucial element in the attempt to coordinate international collaboration, based on the currently accepted rules of traditional warfare."[12] Ganor further states that *"an objective definition to terrorism is not only possible; it is also indispensable to any serious attempt to combat terrorism."* (Emphasis added.)
- **Eqbal Ahmad**[13] discusses the manner in which official definitions of terrorism do not define it, but rather "explain it, express it emotively, polemically, to arouse our emotions rather than exercise our intelligence." He also believes that the definition of terrorism must be fair and leave out motivation.[14]

continued on next page

---

11. Dr. Boaz Ganor is the founder of the International Policy Institute for Counter-Terrorism. His Ph.D. thesis was on "Israel's Counter-Terrorism Strategy" and he served as a consultant to Israeli Government Ministries on Counter-Terrorism.

12. "Defining Terrorism: Is One Man's Terrorist Another Man's Freedom Fighter?" *available at* http://ictconference.org/var/119/17070-Def%20Terrorism%20by%20Dr.%20Boaz%20Ganor.pdf/.

13. Eqbal Ahmad was a Pakistani writer, journalist and anti-war activist who passed away in 1999. He graduated from Forman Christian College in Lahore, Pakistan with a degree in economics. He later studied political science and Middle Eastern history at Princeton University.

14. "Genesis of International Terrorism," *available at* http://www.hartford-hwp.com/archives/27d/083.html.

- **Major Robert W. Cerney, USMC:**[15] "The gross inability of the international community to agree on even the definition of terrorism is indicative of why terrorism is so successful. The United States is as much to blame as any nation with our continually oscillating policies of support depending on what benefits us most."[16]
- Middle East leaders insist on a definition of terrorism, specifically one that excludes those individuals and groups whose motives are nationalist/liberation.

No
- As Cerney points out, terrorists are the least likely criminals to be caught and prosecuted. Though Cerney argues for a definition of terrorism that recognizes it as a form of warfare (as opposed to a mere crime), his point about the inability of governments to prosecute terrorists leads to the conclusion that perhaps the focus should shift from success at the prosecution level to success at the deterrence/incapacitation level.
- **W. Michael Reisman:**[17] "Any consideration of the range of lawful responses to international terrorism, the policymaker and adviser should eschew rather narrowly bounded a priori definitions of terrorism as well as unexamined assumptions about the marginality or inherent lack of utility of terrorism. It will be useful to look, instead, at the full range of possible authors of terrorism, assessing what contemporary international law has prescribed and should prescribe with respect to responses to each of them in such a way as to address the dangers international terrorism poses to world order."[18]

Maybe
- **Lucy Martinez**[19] argues that the lack of definitional consensus is not "in itself an obstacle to the ICC exercising jurisdiction over terrorists. The real issue is whether individual terrorist acts, as opposed to an abstract concept of terrorism, can be prosecuted at the ICC."[20]

continued on next page

---

15. Robert Cerney is a Major with the United States Marine Corps. He serves with the Marine Corps University Command and Staff College.

16. "International Terrorism: The Poor Man's Warfare," *available at* http://www.globalsecurity.org/military/library/report/1991/CRW.htm/.

17. W. Michael Reismann is a professor of law at Yale Law School. He has been a visiting professor in Tokyo, Hong Kong, Berlin, Basel, Paris, and Geneva. He is a member of the Advisory Committee on International Law of the Department of State.

18. *International Legal Responses to Terrorism,* HOUSTON JOURNAL OF INTERNATIONAL LAW Vol. 22, 1999.

19. Lucy Martinez is an associate in law who received her degree from Columbia Law School. She received her bachelor's degree, with honors, from University of Queensland in Australia.

20. *Prosecuting Terrorists at the International Criminal Court: Possibilities and Problems,* RUTGERS L.J., Fall 2002.

- **Charles Ruby**[21] discusses differing perspectives to emphasize that even with a firm definition, different people can interpret an act differently. Therefore, one should choose a "behavioral" model whereby terrorism is defined purely by the behaviors involved, regardless of the laws or morality of those doing the defining. Under this paradigm, different interpreters will necessarily arrive at the same conclusion as to whether something was terrorism, and therefore this method is the most reliable.[22]
- **Reuven Young**[23] argues that there is also a "common law" international definition of terrorism that can be discerned from different parts of international law; therefore, continuing to define terrorism is not necessary.[24]
- **Jason Burke**[25] in *Al Qaeda:* "There are multiple ways of defining terrorism, and all are subjective. Most define terrorism as 'the use or threat of serious violence to advance some kind of cause.' Some state clearly the kinds of group ('subnational,' 'non-state') or cause (political, ideological, religious) to which they refer. Others merely rely on the instinct of most people when confronted with innocent civilians being killed or maimed by men armed with explosives, firearms of other weapons. None is satisfactory, and grave problems with the use of the term persist. Terrorism is, after all, a tactic. The term 'war on terrorism' is thus effectively nonsensical. As there is no space here to explore this involved and difficult debate, my preference is, on the whole, for the less loaded term 'militancy.' This is not an attempt to condone such actions, merely to analyze them in a clear way."[26]

It is possible that the "need" to define terrorism depends on the definition itself. Maybe there is a need to define terrorism uniformly in order to facilitate global cooperation. Perhaps domestic definitions should be flexible (or quasi non-existent) in order to enable countries to respond to terrorism according to their respective laws and circumstances. This, obviously, contributes to unclarity, if not amorphousness, which has strategic significance. As an example, perceived excess — based in part on a lack of definitional rigor — has impacted international cooperation with the U.S. following 9/11. While some may argue that other countries are hesitant *in any event* to cooperate with the U.S., there is

---

21. Charles Ruby is a clinical psychologist at the Pinnacle Center for Mental Health and Human Relations.
22. *The Definition of Terrorism*, ANALYSES OF SOCIAL ISSUES AND PUBLIC POLICY 2 (1), 9-14 (2002).
23. Reuven B. Young is an associate in Davis Polk & Wardwell's Corporate Department and works in the firm's London office.
24. *Defining Terrorism: The Evolution of Terrorism as a Legal Concept in International Law and Its Influence on Definitions In Domestic Legislation*, 29 B.C. INT'L & COMP. L. REV. 23 (2006).
25. Jason Burke is the chief foreign correspondent of *The Observer*, a British newspaper. He covered the wars in Afghanistan and Iraq.
26. AL-QAEDA: THE TRUE STORY OF RADICAL ISLAM (I.B. Tauris, 2004).

little doubt that Guantanamo (as an example of definitional uncertainty) has enormously exacerbated that hesitation.

The definition suggested above addresses two critical issues of terrorism—the importance of the cause as motivation for acting, and the civilian population as the random target of violent acts (including property damage in addition to the loss of life) and non-violent acts (including intimidating civilians from conducting their normal, daily activity). A clear definition such as the one proposed seeks to ensure that collateral damage is minimized. To that end, terrorism should be defined to ensure legal, moral, and effective counterterrorism.

F. DEFINING COUNTERTERRORISM

The term "counterterrorism" must be viewed from two separate, yet equally important, perspectives: state actions responding directly to terrorists and terrorist organizations (reactive and proactive), and state actions attempting to limit a terrorist organization's potential recruitment pool (proactive).

Counterterrorism is defined as:

> The actions of a state, proactive or reactive, intended to kill or injure terrorists and/or to cause serious significant damage to the terrorist's infrastructure *and* refinancing (financing) of socioeconomically depressed regions of the world, and educating communities regarding democracy and its values.

1. Developing a Counterterrorism Strategy

Counterterrorism is a never-ending war of attrition conducted in baby steps comprised of victories and defeats alike. Counterterrorism must be understood in terms of domestic legislation, international law, judicial activism, intelligence gathering, and interrogation of detainees. A workable definition of counterterrorism addresses how and when to act—and against whom.

Counterterrorism demands recognition of critical attributes of actionable intelligence, operational capability, and an understanding that swift victory is, at best, a fiction. Counterterrorism in civil democratic societies must also be conducted according to the rule of law and morality in armed conflict.

Counterterrorism must constantly be couched in terms of defining "effectiveness," which will be discussed at length in Chapter 10. The quality and success of counterterrorism is ultimately determined by whether or not the actions, responses, and operations are effective.

QUESTIONS TO CONSIDER

1. Does killing a particular terrorist indicate success?
2. Should success be defined in a short-term or long-term context, tactically or strategically?
3. Do politics rule the day, meaning that a show of power is the preferred means, as opposed to piecemeal, consistent attacks on identified terrorist targets?
4. Are all individuals involved in the terrorist network legitimate targets?
5. What is the status of the financiers of terrorism?

Effectiveness in counterterrorism is a matter of much disagreement, if not controversy. I propose that operational counterterrorism is *effective* if the terrorist infrastructure suffers serious damage, thereby preventing a particular, planned attack from going forth and postponing or impacting plans for future attacks. While terrorism cannot be defeated, the tactical impact of preventive measures should not be minimized.

A counterterrorism policy must also consider limitations predicated on balancing legitimate national security interests and the rights of the individual. How that balance is maintained, from the perspective of both law and policy, must be analyzed in the context of both terrorist threats and actual attacks. To that end, an effective operational counterterrorism policy must be based on risk and threat assessment alike.

2. Three Models

States' efforts to create counterterrorist policies that adhere to international legal norms have resulted in different approaches. Arunabha Bhoumik, in an analysis of counterterrorist policy, notes that the criminal justice, intelligence, and war models present three legitimate paradigms to shape international counterterrorist policy. For Bhoumik, a proper definition of counterterrorism necessarily involves these three models.[27]

The *criminal model* excludes the international community to some extent by largely incorporating only domestic efforts. The criminal model morally condemns terrorist actions, is legitimate, and is not

---

27. Arunabha Bhoumik, *Democratic Responses to Terrorism: A Comparative Study of the United States, Israel, and India*, 33 DENV. J. INT'L L. & POL'Y 285, 299 (2005).

prone to human rights abuses. However, since it is reactive, rather than preventative, the criminal justice model does not offer the same protections as other counterterrorism policies.

In the *intelligence model*, the suspect is no longer merely a criminal, but rather presents a threat to international security. The intelligence model is not constrained by the procedural constraints of the criminal law model, but it does pose a danger of violating individual civil rights.

Finally, the *war model* facilitates a proactive, sometimes preemptive action against wider population bases — usually a state. The war model may create significant collateral damage and may destabilize foreign governments that are considered terrorist supporters (to varying degrees). It generally infringes on individual civil liberties, may involve profiling, and ultimately may engender terrorist responses rather than preventing them.

G. CONCLUSION

Justifiable counterterrorist action must be subject to some legal norms. Human Rights Watch has commented that "with the advent of the 'war on terror,' governments are increasingly employing counterterrorism measures that themselves violate basic human rights. Such approaches to counterterrorism are not only wrong and illegal, but also shortsighted and counterproductive. Experience suggests that human rights abuses committed in the name of counterterrorism serve to fuel terrorism, not to reduce it."[28]

What price is democracy willing to pay for security? Society must answer this question. The legislative and judicial branches, local government officials, the media, and the public have the responsibility to hold the executive accountable for its counterterrorism measures. Otherwise, human rights violations and ineffective operational counterterrorism are inevitable.

---

28. Human Rights Watch, Counterterrorism, http://hrw.org/doc/?t=ct (last visited Nov. 28, 2007).

CHAPTER 2

WHAT MOTIVATES THE TERRORIST?

A. INTRODUCTION

Understanding what motivates the terrorist is critical to understanding terrorism. Psychologists, sociologists, philosophers, religious experts, political scientists, counterterrorism experts, and even terrorists themselves have all written on this complex and compelling topic. Motivation might best be defined as the sum total of factors that drive an individual to commit certain acts. Terrorists are driven to act by a variety of factors, known and unknown, and we must therefore employ a multidisciplinary approach in trying to understand their motives and rationale.

While serving in the Israel Defense Force (IDF), I prosecuted, remanded into custody, acquitted, convicted, and sentenced an extraordinarily wide range of individuals from the West Bank and Gaza Strip. These individuals—male and female, of all ages and circumstances—had been arrested for suspected terrorist activity ranging from throwing stones and Molotov cocktails at cars, to killing Israelis and fellow Palestinians suspected of collaborating with Israel.

Intensive interaction with thousands of such suspects provided an important insight—namely, that while there are certain common traits among terrorists (extreme dedication to a cause, primarily), the answers each suspect could provide to the question of "Why?" revealed that there is no one homogenous terrorist mind-set, and that motivations to act were as varied as the individuals themselves.

B. DEDICATION

Among those I prosecuted, remanded, and tried were either suspects who had been wanted by the IDF and the General Security Services

(GSS), or apprehended in the act. The wanted terrorist illustrates a critical theme in the study of terrorism — absolute dedication to a cause. The hardships involved in a life spent perpetually evading capture can be endured only by the most dedicated and driven of individuals.

Wanted terrorists are in constant search of safe harbor, both from security forces trying to arrest them and from collaborators seeking to provide the security services information as to their whereabouts. One of the greatest challenges facing the wanted terrorist is identifying who in his own camp might betray him. That fear alone keeps the terrorist moving from hide-out to hide-out, from safe house to safe house. Constantly changing sleeping locations and habits is complicated and difficult to sustain. Attempting to maintain contact with family members not only requires significant logistic coordination, but also increases the possibility of either being spotted or of having those family members detained and interrogated by the security forces.

In Israel, such an interrogation is legal provided it is limited to seeking particulars regarding the suspect: known hiding places, modus operandi, and individuals providing him or her logistical support. It is illegal if the interrogation is used to harm or make threats to family members in an effort to detain the suspect. Yet the constant possibility of a violent interrogation of a parent, spouse, sibling, or child must weigh heavily on the mind of the terrorist.

The wanted terrorist is also in constant physical danger. If security services identify the individual, they will likely shoot to kill. A terrorist is also subject to the hardships imposed by topography, geography, and the environment. He does not have the freedom of mobility someone else might enjoy — trips to the doctor involve the same challenges as seeing family members.

This is not to idealize or empathize with the struggle that a wanted terrorist endures, but rather to explain the degree of motivation required to dedicate oneself to the cause. An individual terrorist's commitment to a cause must be absolute, particularly once security forces learn of his or her identity. In the same way that not all soldiers are suited to be members of the elite Navy SEALS, not all terrorists are equipped to handle the extreme hardships of such a life.

C. THE "EXTRA" FACTOR

Why do some individuals choose to become terrorists? Why do others not? What are the factors that contribute to someone desiring to serve the cause above all and believing that any sacrifice is justified? There is no single, simple answer.

Walter Laqueur's comments on the subject of terrorist motivation are particularly insightful:

> Many terrorisms exist, and their character has changed over time and from country to country. The endeavor to find a "general theory" of terrorism, one overall explanation of its roots, is a futile and misguided enterprise.[1]

Dedication to a cause is what drives individuals, from those merely offering passive support to terrorist groups to those who actually carry out suicide bombings. But a cause alone does not compel every supporter to commit terrorist acts. For example, many people may support an independent state of X, but go through the political process to achieve this goal, while others resort to terrorism.

GOAL: ACHIEVING SELF-RULE FOR THE PEOPLE OF STATE X	
Method: Passive resistance — economic boycotts, peaceful demonstrations, hunger strikes, etc.	Method: Terrorist attacks — suicide bombing campaigns, bomb threats, anthrax scares, etc.

This is not to say that terrorist groups never utilize lawful tactics to achieve their goals, or that legitimate groups will forever refrain from terrorist activity. Yet the line, indefinable at times, does exist. Students of terrorist movements must ask themselves what it is that motivates one group to employ legitimate processes while another group engages in illegitimate means, even though their belief in a particular cause is similar. What are the "extra factors" that, when added to a cause, drive an individual to commit acts of terrorism?

Examining different terrorist organizations helps to effectively explain various motivations. The terrorist organizations included in the chart below represent a cross-section of movements, nationalities, means, and aspirations. All, however, are composed of some individuals willing to die for the cause, others who supply only passive support, and some who provide logistic and financial support.

---

1. WALTER LACQUER, NO END TO WAR: TERRORISM IN THE TWENTY-FIRST CENTURY 22 (2004).

FIGURE 2.1   Different Types of Terrorist Groups = Different Motivations at Play

MOTIVATOR	EXAMPLES
Ideological Motivators: In the 1960s and 70s, nations were confronted with radical left-wing terrorism.	Germany's **Baader-Meinhof**, whose motivation was "fighting a West German capitalist establishment which they (the members) apparently believed was little more than a reincarnation of the Third Reich," was responsible for killing leading industrialist Hanns Martin Schleyer.
	Italy's **Red Brigade** sought to "create a revolutionary state through armed struggle and to separate Italy from the Western Alliance." The group was responsible for the death of political leaders such as former Italian Prime Minister Aldo Moro.
	Similarly in Japan, the **Red Army** sought to "overthrow the Japanese Government and monarchy and to help foment world revolution." The Red Army was responsible for the Lod (Israel) Airport attack, which killed 26 people (largely Puerto Rican pilgrims traveling to Israel during Christmas) and wounded 78.
Nationalist Motivators	The **Shining Path** in Peru seeks "to topple the existing Peruvian government and impose (its) own communist regime." To that end, the organization carried our indiscriminate attacks resulting in the deaths of over 30,000 people.
	In Sri Lanka, the **Liberation Tigers of Tamil Eelam** seek an "independent state in areas in Sri Lanka inhabited by ethnic Tamils." The Tigers have "used conventional, guerrilla, and terror tactics, including some 200 suicide bombings, in a bloody, two-decade-old civil war that has claimed more than 60,000 lives and displaced hundreds of thousands of Sri Lankans."
Personal Motivators (Revenge/ Hatred)	**Timothy McVeigh**, who was responsible for the Oklahoma City bombing (which killed 168 people and wounded over 800), was largely a one-man show, though he was associated with the Michigan Militia (as was Terry Nichols, who assisted McVeigh). What motivated McVeigh was a

continued on next page

MOTIVATOR	EXAMPLES
	hatred of the U.S. government and a desire for revenge regarding two events: 1. The deaths of 86 members of the Branch Davidian cult that resulted when the FBI attempted to end a 68-day stand-off in Waco, Texas 2. Ruby Ridge, Idaho, where an FBI siege of the compound of an Aryan Nation sympathizer, Randy Weaver, resulted in the deaths of Weaver's wife and child.

Membership of the above-mentioned groups ranges from the tens to the thousands. Motivators like ideology and nationalism can draw higher numbers than more personal motivators. While Timothy McVeigh was loosely affiliated with the Michigan Militia, it would be incorrect to suggest that the Oklahoma City bombing was an act of terrorism committed on behalf of that organization. At the same time, while McVeigh acted largely alone, his actions were significantly different than those of Ted Kaczynski, who not only acted alone but whose cause (anti-progress) may have been affected by schizophrenia.

What, then, ties these dissimilar organizations and members together? Does *anything* tie them together? The disparate goals include the following: establishing a secular, independent state, revenge, killing specific individuals, and the creation of a theocracy. Different goals suggest different motivations. Yet all groups contain individuals who are willing to either kill or die for their cause.

It is important to note that the chart generalizes to a degree. No one motivating factor — nationalism, world revolution, revenge — is the cause of an individual's actions. Many cite religion as the primary motivator of terrorism in the modern era, but this might oversimplify the issue. Conventional wisdom suggests that suicide bombing is the exclusive domain of religiously motivated terrorism, but political scientist Robert Pape argues otherwise. Citing the secular Tamil Tigers as the leading perpetrators of suicide attacks, Pape suggests that suicide terrorism is mainly employed by nationalist-driven groups who are fighting a "foreign occupation."[2]

It would be incorrect to argue that motivations are mutually exclusive, even though goals may be distinctly dissimilar. While different

---

2. Robert Pape, *Blowing Up an Assumption*, N.Y. TIMES, May 18, 2005, at A23.

motivations may drive the individual terrorist, the goal is usually surprisingly similar. Ultimately, all terrorist groups have a common goal — to be rid of a particular social or political order. The difference lies in what they want to replace it with.

D. TERRORIST MANIFESTOS

Terrorists often take great pains to rationalize their behavior, drafting charters and manifestos to justify their actions within societal norms.[3] The manifestos issued by terrorist organizations strongly suggest a willingness — actually a commitment — to perform deadly acts on behalf of movements dedicated to causes such as "changing the world," "establishing a separate state," "punishing capitalist societies and their mainstays," and others.

- Palestinian Islamic Jihad: Rejects "any peaceful solution to the Palestinian cause, and the affirmation of the Jihad solution and the martyrdom style as the only choice for liberation."

- Al Qaeda: "We vow by the name of God that we are determined to destroy the American empire....Doctrine and mission are clear and they can be summarized as our agreement to believe in and fight for the religion of God. We believe that those who follow these beliefs and the provisions of faith are true Muslims and anyone who denounces any of these believes and conditions is an infidel even if he still claims to be a Muslim....The call for jihad goes on until doomsday, whether there is an imam calling for it or not."

- Yasser Arafat: "We plan to eliminate the state of Israel and establish a purely Palestinian state. We will make life unbearable for the Jews by psychological warfare and population explosion....We Palestinians will take over everything, including all of Jerusalem."

- Provisional Irish Republican Army's 1977 training manual: The strategy of the "Long War" is to "[cause] as many deaths as possible so as to create a demand from [the British people] at home for their withdrawal; a bombing campaign aimed at making the enemy's financial interests in our country unprofitable while at the same time curbing long-term investment in our country."

---

3. *See generally* Thomas J. Badey, *Defining International Terrorism: A Pragmatic Approach*, 10 Terrorism and Political Violence 90 (1998). Article available at http://socsci.colorado.edu/~gyoung/home/3191/terror.htm).

In *Terrorism in the 21st Century*, Cindy Combs argues that there are two types of terrorist groups—those who claim their actions are justifiable and those who reject the notion of morality (and therefore justification itself). In the first group are individuals who commit reprehensible acts, but still adhere to some moral code. In the second group are individuals such as anarchists who reject the notion of a moral code.[4] The individuals in the second group are beyond the scope of the present book. The motivations of those in the first group are at the very heart of it.

Analysis of the motivations of terrorists is made doubly challenging by the tendency of terrorist organizations to speak in generalities that are inherently superficial. An individual dedicated to advancing a cause is willing to commit certain acts. Not all terrorists—active or passive— are willing to kill themselves. What becomes evident in discussions with terrorists is that they are normal people in some basic sense of the word, acting in response to a complex set of motivations. They are not dismissible as simply "crazy" or "fanatical."

Because terrorists cannot simply be dismissed as lunatics, policy makers are faced with a complexity far greater than what they often anticipate. They must understand both individual motivation and group motivation—based, in part, on ideological considerations. Thus developing counterterrorism strategy requires a sophisticated understanding of what particular individuals (as well as groups) are willing to do in order to advance a cause.

E. HATRED AND REVENGE

Understanding the root causes of hatred is critical for policy makers seeking to develop viable counterterrorism strategies. According to IDF intelligence sources, there are two critical motivators for Palestinian suicide bombers. First, the desire to seek revenge against Israel and Israelis for humiliations suffered by family members, particularly at IDF-manned checkpoints[5] in the West Bank and Gaza Strip.[6] The second motivator is a sense of despair resulting from the Palestinian economic and social condition, particularly in the Gaza Strip.

---

4. CINDY C. COMBS, TERRORISM IN THE 21ST CENTURY (2003).

5. This was one of the primary reasons why the IDF School of Military Law created an interactive video teaching junior commanders how to conduct themselves with respect to the civilian population in "armed conflict short of war." For an article detailing the pedagogy of the interactive video, *see* Amos N. Guiora, *Teaching Morality in Armed Conflict: The Israel Defense Forces Model*, 18 JEWISH POL. STUD. REV. at 3 (2006).

6. This book is written both after the IDF disengaged from the Gaza Strip (2006) and Hamas' deposing the Palestinian Authority in the Gaza Strip (2007).

While the reader may consider these reasons to be an oversimplification, available intelligence indicates the veracity of these two motivators. While other psychological and ideological reasons may also be at play, it is possible that a primary motivator may be basic human desire for revenge for a wrong done to a loved one.

revenge

EXAMPLE

> In countless remand hearings of individuals suspected of terrorist activity, I found myself asking, "Why?" Why did you attack such and such? The worthiness of the question is much debated, but the question is relevant to discerning motivation. Even when suspects offer a vaguely formed response akin to "I hate all...," the answer is instructive. It illustrates the impact, power, and significance of "hate."

Is simple hatred a strong enough motivation to randomly kill innocent people, including children? A suicide bombing is the ultimate expression of dedication to a cause. Not only does the actor lose his or her life in this final act, but immediately preceeding detonation, a suicide bomber is in the physical presence of individuals about to be killed. He or she is able to look at the randomly selected victims in the eye seconds before killing them.

Hanadi Jaradat was a twenty-eight year old attorney who killed 21 people in a suicide bombing in a Haifa restaurant after being dispatched by Islamic Jihad. A few years prior to the bombing, Jaradat witnessed the targeted killing of her fiancé by Israeli security forces. There have also been reports that undercover IDF operatives killed her younger brother and a cousin the evening before her brother's wedding. Her desire to exact revenge was so powerful that according to her handlers—who, for reasons unknown, had apparently tried to convince her to not carry out the attack—there was "no stopping her." What does this suggest with respect to that individual's motivations?

F. PSYCHOLOGY

The psychological make-up of an individual clearly influences his or her decision to engage in acts of terrorism. Applied generically, however, psychology can oversimplify a complex issue, leading policy makers to reach faulty conclusions about how to react to acts of terrorism whose ultimate causes may remain obscure. Nevertheless, research suggests there is often a significant psychological component to terrorist motivation. If terrorist motivation is the result of a combination of several factors, then individual psychology can only be one of those.

Psychologist Ronnie Janoff-Bulman argues that there are three fundamental human assumptions that under normal circumstances generally go unquestioned — benevolence, meaningfulness of the world, and self-worth. She suggests that when psychological trauma occurs, it challenges these assumptions, sometimes shattering them beyond repair.[7]

In discussing the impact of psychological trauma on suicide bombers, Anne Speckhard and Khapta Akhmedova note that, common perception aside, psychological trauma is not the same as mental illness. Speckhard and Akhmedova define a traumatizing experience as "an inescapable, horrifying and terrifying experience which is life threatening or threatens serious injury, or in which a person witnesses or learns of the death or serious injury of another."[8] Speckhard and other researchers have suggested that such individuals are particularly susceptible to terrorist recruiters.

Speckhard argues that two different factors motivate an individual to become a suicide bomber following psychological trauma.[9]

INDIVIDUALS WITHIN ZONES OF ACTIVE CONFLICT	INDIVIDUALS OUTSIDE ACTIVE ZONES OF CONFLICT
Outward Characteristics: Often nationalistic, view the conflict in terms of self and community defense, attempting to mete out justice to a perceived enemy occupier.	Outward Characteristics: Influenced by activities within zones of conflict by Internet images, video footage, pictures and propaganda, some individuals can develop a deep sense of secondary traumatization despite the fact that they themselves have not suffered any direct injury or deprivation.

continued on next page

---

7. Ronnie Jannof-Bulman, Shattered Assumptions: Towards a New Psychology of Trauma (1992).

8. Anne Speckhard & Khapta Akhmedova, *The New Chechen Jihad: Militant Wahhabism as a Radical Movement and a Source of Suicide Terrorism in Post-War Chechen Society*, 2 Democracy & Security 1, 41 (2006). *See also* Anne Speckhard & Khapta Akhmedova, *Black Widows and Beyond: Understanding the Motivations and Life Trajectories of Chechen Female Suicide Terrorists* in Women Terrorists and Militants: Agency, Utility and Organization (Cindy Ness ed., 2007).

9. Anne Speckhard. *Understanding Suicide Terrorism: Countering Human Bombs and Their Senders*, in Topics in Terrorism: Toward a Transatlantic Consensus on the Nature of the Threat, Vol. 1. (Jason S. Purcell & Joshua D. Weintraub eds., 2005), available at http://www.annespeckhard.com/publications/Suicide_Terrorism_Countering_Human_Bombs.pdf.

INDIVIDUALS WITHIN ZONES OF ACTIVE CONFLICT	INDIVIDUALS OUTSIDE ACTIVE ZONES OF CONFLICT
Psychological Characteristics: Deeply dissociative and even refer to themselves as "already dead."	Psychological Characteristics: Generally vulnerable to terrorist ideologies due to a sense of alienation, marginalization and lack of positive identity.

EXAMPLE

Consider "Pioneers of Tomorrow," a weekly children's program on Hamas TV, which featured characters including Saraa and Sanabel, two young girls who discuss "annihilating the Jews" and "committing martyrdom," and Farfour, a Mickey Mouse–like character who is entrusted with his family's land by his dying grandfather. In the final episode of "Pioneers of Tomorrow," Farfour is beaten to death by an Israeli official trying to buy the land. Saraa later explains Farfour's death to viewers by saying he was "martyred while defending his land" by "the murderers of innocent children."[10]

Could regularly viewing such a program as a child result in the type of "secondary traumatization" described by Speckhard? If so, what other types of motivators could combine with this psychological trauma to result in an individual turning to terrorism?

Three factors—injustice, identity, and belonging—have been found to strongly influence decisions to join terrorist organizations and engage in terrorist activity. Some analysts have suggested that, regardless of ideology, the synergistic effect of these dynamics form the real "root cause" of terrorism.[11] Former CIA psychiatrist Jerrold Post has similarly theorized that "the need to belong, the need to have a stable identity, to resolve a split and be at one with oneself and with society...is an important bridging concept which helps explain the similarity in behavior of terrorists in groups of widely different espoused motivations and composition."[12]

---

10. *Farfour Mouse Dies in Last Episode*, MIDEAST.JPOST.COM, June 29, 2007, available at http://www.jpost.com/servlet/Satellite?cid=1183053066461&pagename=JPost/JPArticle/ShowFull.

11. *See* Robert Luckabaugh *et al.*, *Terrorist Behavior and U.S. Foreign Policy: Who Is the Enemy? Some Psychological and Political Perspectives*, 34 PSYCHOLOGY 1-15 (1997), concluding, "The real cause or psychological motivation for joining is the great need for belonging, a need to consolidate one's identity. A need to belong, along with an incomplete personal identity, is a common factor that cuts across the groups."

12. Jerrold M. Post, *Notes on a Psychodynamic Theory of Terrorist Behavior*, 7 STUD. IN CONFL. & TERRORISM 241-256 (1984).

Family dynamics can play into the psychology of terrorism as well. In seeking to establish counterterrorism policy, it is important to understand the depth of family and community support many terrorists enjoy. Terrorists can achieve hero-like status in their communities, a fact that supports terrorists and promotes the recruitment of others. What motivates a family—in spite of hardships it may be forced to endure as a consequence—to support a family member in a mission designed to injure and kill civilians? What motivates a family to support a child, sibling, or parent whose mission becomes self-destruction in a suicide bombing? Is it possible that the tramautization described by psychologists can be a family- or even community-wide phenomenon? Is it possible that the need to belong can be exacerbated by a given community? Policy makers must ask these questions if they are to design effective counterterrorism strategy.

Are these psychological explanations the best approach to understanding terrorist motivation? It is possible that, in the case of some terrorists, psychological motivators are not present at all.

Martha Crenshaw addresses the difficulty of demanding an unambiguous "terrorist profile," or a list of characteristics that permit the identification of current or potential terrorists. She points to Andrew Silke's criticism of psychologists who offer "diagnos[es] at a distance," saying that giving terrorists labels like "narcissistic" is misleading and a result of bias. Crenshaw also discusses the often wildly different psychological labels applied to male and female terrorists, with psychiatrists and the public alike attributing mental illness to female terrorists more often than to male terrorists. Crenshaw argues that "terrorism has an autonomous logic that is comprehensible, however unconventional."[13]

Psychology, though imprecise, is perceived as a more familiar and accepted field of inquiry, which makes it more appealing to policy and decision makers. A more complex paradigm—ideology—offers a deeper understanding of the factors that motivate individuals to act, but offers less-than-tidy answers to those who must conceive and execute counterterrorism policies.

Without disregarding the importance of psychology, we must conclude that motivation extends beyond psychology alone. Psychology may be *a* factor, but is very clearly not *the* factor. To view terrorism from a more sophisticated and subtle perspective, ideological motivations must also be examined.

---

13. Martha Crenshaw, *The Psychology of Terrorism: An Agenda for the 21st Century*, 21 POLITICAL PSYCHOLOGY 405, 410 (2000).

G. IDEOLOGY

Webster's Dictionary defines ideology as a "manner or the content of thinking characteristic of an individual, group, or culture." Ideology comprises an individual's entire worldview — beliefs, attitudes, and values that the individual believes apply to all aspects of life. Terrorist ideology should be viewed from three different perspectives: nationalism, religion, and either left-wing Marxism or right-wing fascism. The first two are particularly pertinent to our discussion because left- and right-wing terrorism have both decreased markedly in recent decades.

1. Nationalism/Separatism

Throughout recent history, many terrorist organizations have been motivated by the goal of creating an independent state based on ethnic or nationalistic identities. In 1945 the United Nations Charter came into force, stating that the purposes of the UN include the promotion of self-determination.[14] What exactly "self-determination" means has been an issue international law has subsequently addressed.

Many terrorist organizations point to the UN Charter, as well as more recent international covenants including the International Covenant on Civil and Political Rights, which states "all peoples have the right of self-determination," as justification for their actions. These arguments have been used by the Liberation Tigers of Tamil Eelam in its fight against the Sri Lankan government; the Kurdish Workers Party in the fight for the creation of an independent state of Kurdistan in parts of Turkey, Iran, Iraq, and Syria; the Provisional Irish Republican Army in the struggle to unify Northern Ireland with the Republic of Ireland; the Basque National and Liberty organization, which fights for the creation of a Basque state in parts of Spain and France; the Palestinian Liberation Organization in its fight against the state of Israel; and Chechen nationalists, who seek a Chechen state separate from Russia, among others.

Nationalist-based terrorists attempt to forge national identity by appealing to the background of a particular ethnic group. Violence may be deemed particularly effective at achieving this. When a government responds with force to a terrorist act, it draws attention to the group, allowing terrorists to present themselves as victims. Historically this has increased public awareness, and financial and social support for the cause. Moral outrage on the part of the attacked state, therefore, may have the

---

14. U.N. Charter, art. 1, para. 2, available at http://www.un.org/aboutun/charter/.

ironic impact of creating more cohesion among members of the ethnic group to which the terrorists belong.

Nationalistic terrorists tend to have greater longevity than terror groups whose motivations are philosophy-based, such as Marxist or fascist groups. Confronted with a terror group whose motivations are based on nationalism or ethnic separatism, policy makers can seek to empower the ethnic community to work within the current political system. Doing so encourages self-policing, thereby possibly winning over moderates within the political system. This policy succeeded in Northern Ireland, where the Provisional Irish Republican Army underwent organizational changes in response to moderates within the group breaking off. A ceasefire was declared in the late 1990s when Sinn Fein (the political branch of the group) was admitted to peace talks, which ultimately produced the Belfast Agreement of 1998. The difficulty policy makers face is how to empower the ethnic community effectively without simply appeasing the violent element of separatists.

However, when nationalism and religion combine to form a single potent motivation, finding the middle ground lending itself to compromise may become extremely difficult. Religion as understood and practiced by true believers does not brook compromise.

2. Religion as Ideology

Political ideologies—self-determination, creating an ideal economic or political regime—are more readily understood than religious ideologies as motivators of terrorism. While religion has undoubtedly been a prime motivator for acts of violence and conflicts throughout history, it has not been associated with terrorism until recently. The political ideologies previously referred to were the primary motivators for terrorism in decades past, but they have since been surpassed by religion.

As noted earlier, there is no single motivation to commit terrorism. Religious-based terrorism is invariably mixed with the personal and political motivators previously discussed. Religion as ideology is today the most dynamic motive behind acts of terrorism that this generation—and possibly future generations—will face.

The concept of religion is expansive, and to claim that terrorists are motivated solely by religion does not offer much help in understanding either religion or terrorism. Terrorists can be driven to act by different aspects of the very same religion—a Muslim suicide bomber could be motivated by the promise of paradise, the forgiveness for sins committed in this life, the restoration of family honor, or contribution to God's holy cause on earth. To say that religion is the driving force in all these different instances is true, but not specific enough. To better understand how religion can inspire terrorism, therefore, we must seek a deeper understanding of the way in which the adherents of various faiths conceive of religion.

A discussion of religion and terrorism should not become a criticism of Islam. Christians and Jews have similarly committed acts of violence attributed to divine inspiration and religious belief. Crusaders sought to "liberate" the Holy Land; radical right-wing Christian groups bombed gay nightclubs and abortion clinics; Yigal Amir claimed he was carrying out the will of God when he assassinated Israeli Prime Minister Yitzhak Rabin.

But while terrorism has been committed in the names of all three monotheistic religions, religiously inspired suicide bombings have only been carried out by Islamic terrorists to date. As suicide bombings are the ultimate expression of a terrorist's motivation, the following discussion will focus on Islam, but can be applied to all religiously motivated terrorists.

Whether the act is committed in response to the teachings of a rabbi, a priest, or an imam, acting in the name of God is a critical motivation for Jews, Christians, and Muslims alike. The concept of duty and obligation to God is paramount in the religious-based terrorism paradigm. This then begets the question: How does religion so effectively motivate? After all, do not all three major monotheistic religions—Christianity, Islam, Judaism—preach messages of compassion, charity, and selflessness? How, then, have all three been used as the basis for violence against other individuals? Has religion been perverted for political purposes, or is religion itself inherently violent?

If religion is not inherently evil, how is it that religious scripture is used to exhort devout followers to kill the "other"? Has compassionate religion been replaced by the religion of hate? If so, how are nation-states to develop viable and lawful counterterrorism policies that address these issues without violating the individual right to practice religion as one chooses? It is not merely the danger of additional religiously motivated terror attacks that nation-states must fear—they must also ensure that harsh policies do not drive moderate practitioners of various religions into the waiting arms of extremists.

a. Fundamentalist Movements

The question of whether religion has been perverted when it is offered as justification for terrorist acts, or whether religion is inherently violent, is mostly irrelevant in the context of fundamentalist religious movements. The "purity" of the religion in question is not as important as how the individual in question views that religion. When an individual subscribes to a fundamentalist view of a faith, this becomes the only view.

Fundamentalists believe in the supreme authority of their scripture — or, at least, what they understand to be their scripture. Whether the 72 vestal virgins promised Islamic suicide bombers are actually described directly in the Qu'ran, or whether they are the product of urban legend, is largely insignificant. Many aspiring suicide bombers believe this much-anticipated award awaits them.

Additionally, since fundamentalists believe that scripture comes directly from God or God's prophets, words are to be taken literally. Since many scriptures contain passages that describe violence and revenge, these words offer both justifications and commandments to the fundamentalist follower. Fundamentalists ascribe to a literalist approach to scripture.

For the actor who believes in the infallibility of her religion, that the act is "done in the name of God" is motivation enough. Whether he or she possesses a profound understanding of religious scripture or doctrine is not important. For example, in the case of Islam, the Qu'ran forbids both murder and suicide. What allows a suicide bomber to justify his or her actions by religion is framing the act in terms of self-sacrifice and martyrdom. Christianity compels followers to "love one another" and "judge not" — yet fundamentalist Christians who bomb abortion clinics or gay clubs are still able to term their actions in terms of devotion to God.

How terrorists view themselves, their enemies, their victims, and the nature of their conflict has a dramatic impact on motivation. To a fundamentalist, members of their religion are among the chosen, the saved. All others are destined for damnation. In a religion that describes everything as "us" and "them," what would otherwise be a purely political fight can literally be framed as a conflict between good and evil.

Thus to the religious terrorist, the victims of an attack are either innocent victims who will fly straight to heaven, or collaborators with evil who deserve their fate. In either case, the actor need not worry about the consequences or their implications. As an agent of God working toward the greater good, a religiously motivated terrorist feels perfectly justified in his or her actions.

b. The Mission

In the context of Islamic religious motivation, the importance of *jihad* cannot be minimized. There is great controversy within the political, academic, and religious communities as to the term's correct definition. *Jihad* literally means "struggle," and has taken on both violent and non-violent meanings. Some Islamic scholars argue that *jihad* is essentially defensive warfare, carried out solely to protect Muslims and Islam. What is clear is that *jihad* has become a rallying call by Islamic terrorist leaders exhorting action against the West, Jews and Muslim non-believers alike. The practical consequence of the contemporary usage and possible manipulation of the term *jihad* is critical to examining motivations, particularly in the fundamentalist setting.

The concept of "the greater good" plays a significant role for terrorists. In innumerable conversations with failed suicide bombers, the repeated refrain was a sense of contribution to the cause—the establishment of a Palestinian state. The sense of mission and the requirement to fulfill it was overwhelmingly how Palestinian detainees would articulate their goals. Many were convinced that their specific action would contribute to the establishment of a Palestinian state. While some suspects lacked sophistication, the sense of commitment was impressive—particularly because intelligence information described the hardship their obligation imposed on their daily lives. While a belief that one act will make a difference may sound quixotic, the depth of commitment suggested that the "party line" had been fully internalized. Suspects were committed to the point of causing pain and suffering to self and family. The power of religiously motivated terrorism is that it knows no borders.

But do all religiously motivated terrorists truly accept the mission? Perhaps not all religiously motivated terrorists are fundamentalists. The promise of eternal reward is appealing not only to the sincere believer, but to desperate people in general. The easy answer to the question of "Why is eternal reward a motivation?" would be that the afterlife presents a positive alternative to the present. When life on earth—whether in the Gaza Strip or Pakistan—is largely devoid of financial or social opportunity, the possibility of an afterlife in paradise (even when not fully believed in) becomes more appealing. Whether this means desperate people are more prone to fundamentalism, or whether desperate people are simply willing to approximate religious fervor in the hope of eternal reward, is a question policy makers must consider.

3. Applying Motivations

Within an organization dedicated to a particular goal, such as a religiously motivated mission, different individuals have distinct roles. It is important to appreciate and recognize gradations and distinctions. The suicide bomber infrastructure includes different categories, all of which are essential to "mission success." These roles likely reflect different degrees of motivation (as well as abilities). The motivations—and strength of conviction—of the suicide bomber (the doer) are different than those of the individuals (senders) who recruited and trained the specific bomber. These motivations are different still from the financier supporting the group, which are distinct from the person whose responsibility it was to drive the bomber to that pizza parlor that within a few minutes will be the site of carnage and death.

All members of the group (bomber, recruiter, financier, driver, logistics manager) share the overarching motivation of the terrorist organization. At the same time, it is obvious that the motivation required to be a suicide bomber is different from that of, for example, the financier.

CHAPTER 3

GEOPOLITICS AND COUNTERTERRORISM

A. INTRODUCTION

Historically, political scientists analyzed geopolitics and international relations in terms of nation-states and coalitions of nation-states. Today, it is clear that non-state actors are capable of contributing to great change both in the domestic affairs of nation-states and across international borders. Therefore terrorism must be examined not only in terms of the individual—who does what, where, when and why?— but also from a macro perspective. To understand terrorism, we must examine it in a broad geopolitical context rather than as an isolated phenomenon.

To do so requires defining geopolitics—*the relationship between a given nation/territory/group/phenomenon and the rest of the world.* When examining terrorism, it is essential that the reader understand that the phenomenon cannot be viewed separately from other strategic, political, economic, social, political, and cultural events. This chapter seeks to explain terrorism in the larger context—how terrorism shapes events beyond one particular attack, and how external events in turn affect terrorism.

We must first determine whether "global Islamic terrorism"—a phrase that has become heavily politicized—is a real phenomenon. It suggests that there is a broad-based movement with largely uniform goals whose intent is to provide religious (Islamic) justification for acts of terrorism both against infidels and secular Arab regimes who have allied with the West. In using the term "Islamic," we do not distinguish between Sunni and Shi'ite Muslims.[1]

---

1. The two main branches of Islam differ mainly in their beliefs about who should succeed the prophet Muhammad to lead the theocracy he had established following his death in 632 A.D. Sunni Muslims believe in choosing a *caliph* by consensus; Shi'ite Muslims believe Muhammad chose his son-in-law Ali as his successor, and that only direct

Does the assertion that global *jihadism* exists promote greater understanding of terrorism? In conversations with Palestinian terrorists from religious and secular organizations alike, it was very clear that they did not see themselves as part of a global terrorist network. Their focus, efforts, and goals were singular — the establishment of a Palestinian state. Those from Hamas and the Islamic Jihad favored a religious Palestinian state, with differing degrees of "religiosity." Those from the PLO, Democratic Front for the Liberation of Palestine, and Popular Front for the Liberation of Palestine favored a secular government. The common denominator was the establishment of a Palestinian state; larger, more global concerns were not raised.

EXAMPLE

The evidence being presented here is admittedly anecdotal and not an empirical study, but the fact remains, in hundreds of conversations when I asked "why," I never once heard "global, Islamic terrorism." The answer was always "Palestinian statehood."

Perhaps politicians and scholars have coined a useless phrase in response to disparate and relatively unconnected acts of terrorism. Suicide bombers are secular and religious alike; however, religious suicide bombers in the modern era are only Muslims. Does that mean that all Islamic suicide bombers — from Hamas, Islamic Jihad, al-Qaeda, Hezbollah, Abu Sayyaf, Chechen separatists, the Tamil Tigers, Kurdistan Workers' Party — are the same? The easy answer is yes. In reality, the answer is no. Different terrorist organizations have distinct goals and different aspirations. It is dangerous from an operational counterterrorism perspective to lump terrorists into one catch-all category.

Geographic-specific terrorist organizations (Hamas) do not share the same goals as global terrorist organizations (al-Qaeda). Therefore, Israel's counterterrorism measures in response to Hamas will differ from the U.S.'s response to al-Qaeda. That is not to suggest that lessons learned from one paradigm are not applicable to another. However, it is important to

---

descendants of Ali and Muhammad's daughter Fatima should rule. The struggle for control between the two groups lasted for decades, with the Shi'ites losing. Sunni Muslims make up about 85-90 percent of the Muslim population worldwide. Yet in the modern era, the primary difference between Sunni and Shi'ite Muslims has more to do with ethnicity and group identity than theology. For more information, see BARNABY ROGERSON, THE HEIRS OF MUHAMMAD: ISLAM'S FIRST CENTURY AND THE ORIGINS OF THE SUNNI-SHIA SPLIT (2007); ALI SHEHATA ET AL., DEMYSTIFYING ISLAM: YOUR GUIDE TO THE MOST MISUNDERSTOOD RELIGION OF THE CENTURY (2007); Dan Murphy, "Islam's Sunni-Shiite Split," CHRISTIAN SCIENCE MONITOR, *available at* http://www.csmonitor.com/2007/0117/p25s01-wome.html.

appreciate that different threats require distinct responses. From a geo-political perspective, the threat Hamas (or any other geographic-specific terrorist organization) presents is quantifiably distinct from the threats posed by a non-geographic specific organization.

B. IS GLOBAL ISLAMIC TERRORISM A GENUINE PHENOMENON?: HAMAS AS A CASE STUDY

Hamas is the largest and most influential militant Palestinian movement today. In Arabic, "hamas" means "zeal," but the word is also an acronym for *Harakat al-Muqawama al-Islamiya*, or "Islamic Resistance Movement." In January 2006, Hamas won the Palestinian Authority's (PA) general legislative elections, defeating Fatah (the party to which the PA's president, Mahmoud Abbas, belongs). In June 2007, Hamas effectively deposed the PA in the Gaza Strip following a series of gun battles between Hamas and the PA's security forces (largely Fatah or PLO).

From a geopolitical perspective, the effect is largely local, rather than international. According to Hamas leadership, the organization is comprised of two separate, independent "wings" — political-social ("cradle to grave") and military (Az al-din Kasem) — dedicated to the establishment of a religious Palestinian state and Israel's destruction.[2] Israel, conversely, argues that Hamas is one organization and its counterterrorism operations are conducted accordingly.

The question addressed in this chapter is whether Hamas's stated purpose to destroy Israel and establish a religious Palestinian state is directly linked to international Islamic terrorism. Since 9/11, it has become conventional wisdom that the world is confronted with "Islamic terrorism" — a unified, global threat. Whether Samuel Huntington's "clash of civilizations" or the phrase "Islamofascism" is the accepted term of art, the suggestion is the same. According to this theory, Islamic extremists are prepared to go to extraordinary means to achieve the following goals: to kill as many Westerners as possible; to cause as much damage to Western assets as possible; and to bring down Arab regimes (Egypt, Jordan, and Saudi Arabia) accused of having allowed the West (particularly the U.S.) to defile Arab society. The range of Islamic terrorism is significant. That does not, however, mean that "international Islamic terrorism" is an absolute truism.

---

2. Hamas Covenant 1998: The Covenant of the Islamic Resistance Movement states that "Israel will exist and will continue to exist until Islam will obliterate it...." *Available at* http://www.yale.edu/lawweb/avalon/mideast/hamas.htm/.

Islamic extremists are committed to the destruction of what Western society most values: democracy, freedom, liberal education, etc. Nevertheless, given the geographic and purpose-specific nature of terrorism, the theory advocating the existence of global Islamic terrorism is a stretch. Some Islamic extremists have a very limited geographical view; others have larger goals. Even when groups share goals, they are not implicitly — much less explicitly — working together. Geographic-specific groups such as Hamas do not seek to destroy the three Arab nations mentioned above. Rather, they are interested solely in local goals of state independence.

In addition, discussing Islam as if it were one unified religion is as misleading as discussing Christianity without making distinctions between Catholics, Protestants, Russian Orthodox, and Greek Orthodox. Different sects in Islam, such as Salafists, do not consider Shiite Muslims to be true believers. For this reason, members of al-Qaeda (Salafists) do not align themselves with members of Hezbollah (Shiites), viewing them as not much better than heathens.

Furthermore, the idea of "global Islamic terrorism" negatively portrays Muslims who do not seek the destruction of the West. The need to cautiously engage in this discussion is critical. Otherwise, dialogue becomes monologue and debate is shouted down by stereotypes.

QUESTIONS TO CONSIDER

1. On whose behalf is Hamas acting?
2. Who is supporting Hamas?
3. What are the motivations of the "foot soldier" willing to blow himself up tomorrow afternoon in a Tel Aviv restaurant?
4. Has Islam been manipulated, if not perverted, by leaders of Hamas? What is the relationship between terrorism and religion?
5. What social and economic conditions are at play?
6. What is the most effective means of reaching out to millions of school-age children taught to hate Western values?
7. What is the responsibility of leaders such as Egyptian President Mubarak in the face of Islamic terrorism?
8. What is the role of European nations facing demographic issues resulting from an open border policy?
9. How much — if at all — is the West expected to "understand" Islamic terrorists?
10. What is the geopolitical significance of two different approaches seeking to attain the same goal?

continued on next page

11. What are the calculations and considerations relevant to the same goal utilizing significantly different methods?
12. How do different methods affect counterterrorism measures?
13. How do the different methods affect the geopolitical considerations of the particular terrorist organization, the directly affected states, the region, and broader interests?

1. On Whose Behalf Is Hamas Acting?

If international terrorism is defined as terrorism advancing a global cause, and were Hamas part of international terrorism, then Hamas members could be perceived to be acting on behalf of a global concept. Conversely, if Hamas is acting on behalf of a local goal, then obviously it is not part of the international terrorism fabric.

In conversations with Hamas leaders and doers ("foot-soldiers") alike, the overwhelming message they articulated was a local mission, related solely to the Palestinian people and therefore unrelated to a larger purpose. The organization was established for the purpose of creating a religious Palestinian state; the internationalization of terrorism is, *at best*, a byproduct from which the organization may benefit. While funds supporting Hamas travel a circuitous international route before arriving at their final destination, that fact does not imply Hamas is inherently a member of the international terrorism "club."

Money is the engine that makes terrorism run. Therefore, any terrorist organization — local and international — is obligated to make every effort to ensure that its coffers are full. Though the financing of terrorism is largely international, the terrorism it supports is not necessarily so. Therefore, while Hamas actively seeks funding from any available source — local or international — the essence of the organization is unaffected.

2. Who Supports Hamas and Why

Hamas is supported by Palestinians who voted for the organization either because of religious devoutness or because they were fed up with the PA's corruption. The organization's core supporters are religious Muslims desirous of a Palestinian state as articulated by Hamas.

Recent reports suggest an attempt both by al-Qaeda and Hezbollah to gain a foothold in the Gaza Strip by sending terrorists to participate in Hamas-led terrorist attacks. However, what has *not* been suggested is that Hamas sent members to Lebanon to fight during the summer of 2006, to

Iraq to assist al-Qaeda, to Afghanistan/Pakistan to assist the Taliban, or to any other location to further a non-Palestinian terrorist effort. The significance of this cannot be minimized — it demonstrates that Hamas is *not* an active participant in external Islamic terrorism (external defined as beyond its immediate geographic region).

3. The Relationship Between Religion and Terrorism

What remains to be discussed is whether Hamas' internal efforts are an integral component of international Islamic terrorism. Perhaps the best way to approach this question is by revisiting the discussion regarding suicide bombers, but in the context of geopolitics. What is the relationship between terrorism and religion? Is religious-based action of Hamas members akin to religious-based action of terrorism elsewhere?

If the answer is affirmative, what is its significance? If a Hamas suicide bomber and another Islamic suicide bomber elsewhere in the world are similarly motivated, in part, by a similar interpretation of the same text, does it follow that both belong to overarching, international Islamic terrorism? Not completely. Both are motivated by the same religious text, but they are not motivated by the same political considerations. *Even* if religion were deemed the primary motivator, that is not enough to suggest that they are acting on behalf of the same cause.

4. Geopolitics and the Local Terror Group

By localizing their terrorist attacks, Hamas has focused exclusively on a specific goal. There are many reasons that might explain Hamas' decision to not take the fight beyond the immediate area. They include the following:

- Hamas lacks the resources to conduct international terrorism (defined as conducting a terrorist campaign beyond a specific region);
- Hamas is unwilling to rely on other groups with greater means and resources. Such reliance would result in becoming indebted or beholden to these more powerful groups who, in return, could demand a "seat at the table" in regard to the West Bank and Gaza Strip;
- Concern about angering states or populations that may otherwise be sympathetic to Hamas' cause;
- Ultimately, Hamas could view its cause as strictly local and prefer to not involve itself in the affairs of outsiders.

Hamas' geopolitical considerations should be compared to the PLO's strategic thinking four decades ago. Such an analysis effectively illustrates different strategies regarding the same goal—establishment of a Palestinian state—predicated on different historical and political considerations. From a strategic perspective, the PLO (established January 1, 1965) determined that the most effective manner to achieve the establishment of a secular Palestinian state was to put the issue on the international map. To that end, the PLO carried out spectacular terrorist acts both inside and outside of Israel. Contrast this with Hamas, which conducts attacks only in the immediate geographic region.

PALESTINE LIBERATION ORGANIZATION: EXAMPLES OF ACTIVITY	HAMAS: EXAMPLES OF ACTIVITY
1968: PLO attacks an El Al airliner in Athens, Greece.	2000: A booby-trapped raft explodes close to an Israeli Navy vessel near the Israel-Egypt border.
1969: Prime Minister of Lebanon allows PLO to recruit, arm, train and employ fighters against Israel in Lebanon. The PLO begins creating a "state within a state" in Lebanon.	2001: A suicide bomber detonated an explosive strapped to his body near an Israeli bus at the French Hill Junction in Jerusalem, wounding 31 Israeli civilians.
1972: Failed hostage-taking attempt at the Munich Olympics result in the deaths of 11 Israeli athletes.	2003: A suicide bomber detonated a bomb in a mall in Netanya. Five Israeli civilians were killed; 86 were wounded.
1978: An attack on a bus and cars on the Tel Aviv-Haifa highway results in the deaths of 35 Israelis and wounds at least 74.	2004: Two suicide bombers detonated a bag of explosives on a No. 19 bus line in Jerusalem. Ten Israelis and one foreigner were killed; 44 were injured.
1982: PLO withdraws from Lebanon and relocates its headquarters in Tunis, Tunisia.	2007: Hamas carries out military operations against PA forces in the streets of Gaza.

Does a state supporting terrorism dictate the methods the organization uses? If so, the following question needs to be asked: If a terrorist organization is the beneficiary of state largesse, does the organization lose its independence, and does that affect its geopolitical considerations and subsequent actions?

That question is relevant not only in the context of state-sponsored terrorism, but also with respect to a geographic-specific terrorist organization being maneuvered, perhaps against its will, to join internationally oriented terrorism. In the Israeli-Palestinian conflict, compare Hamas with the PLO. Hamas rejects inclusion in a larger group, whereas the PLO, which was aligned with the Soviet Union in the Cold War, benefited from Soviet munificence, including arms, equipment, and training.

In the context of the Cold War, the PLO was one of many national liberation movements the Soviet Union supported as part of its larger geopolitical chess-game with the U.S. and its Western allies. To that end, the Soviet Union granted significant largesse to numerous, like-minded national liberation movements with dual goals: geographic-specific (such as the establishment of the State of Palestine) and global (advancing the Soviet Union's larger revolutionary goals). In that sense, the PLO was part of a larger geopolitical puzzle in a manner that Hamas refuses to be.

C. GLOBAL ISLAMIC TERRORISM AND "AL-QAEDA FRANCHISED"

Unlike a local terrorist group such as Hamas, al-Qaeda has a wide range of goals, a fact that is reflected by the range of its targets—within the U.S. (both World Trade Center attacks); American targets outside of United States (embassies in Africa), Western targets in West (Madrid and London); targets outside of the West (Bali nightclub); and Arab regimes that have allowed a U.S. presence (Khobar Towers). See Figure 3.1.

FIGURE 3.1   Al-Qaeda Targets

World Trade Center bombing Feb. 26, 1993	• The WTC in New York City was badly damaged when a car bomb exploded in an underground garage. • Followers of Sheik Omar Abdul Rahman, an Egyptian cleric who preached in the New York City area, were deemed responsible.
Khobar Towers June 25, 1996	• A truck bomb exploded outside the northern perimeter of the U.S. portion of the Khobar Towers housing complex in Saudi Arabia. Nineteen U.S. military personnel were killed; about 500 were wounded. • Several groups claimed responsibility, including Saudi Arabian Hezbollah members with support from the government of Iran.

U.S. Embassy in Kenya August 7, 1998	• A bomb exploded at the rear entrance of the embassy, killing 12 U.S. citizens, 32 Foreign Service Nationals (FSNs) and 247 Kenyan citizens. Approximately 5,000 Kenyans, 13 FSNs and six U.S. citizens were injured. The embassy suffered extensive structural damage. • The U.S. government held Osama bin Laden responsible for the attacks.
U.S. Embassy in Tanzania August 7, 1998	• A bomb exploded outside the embassy, killing seven FSNs and three Tanzanian citizens. The explosion also caused major structural damage to the facility. • The U.S. government held Osama bin Laden responsible for the attacks.
U.S.S. Cole Oct. 12, 2000	• A small dinghy carrying explosives rammed the destroyer, killing 17 soldiers and injuring 39. • Evidence suggests the attack was carried out by Islamic militants wtih possible ties to bin Laden.
September 11, 2001	• Two airliners crashed into the Twin Towers of the WTC. Soon after, the Pentagon was struck by a third plane. A fourth plane, suspected to be bound for a target in Washington, D.C., crashed into a field in southern Pennsylvania. The attacks killed 3,025 U.S. citizens and other nationals. • Al-Qaeda claimed responsibility.
Sari Club Discotheque Oct. 12, 2002	• A car bomb exploded outside a nightclub in Bali, killing 202 and injuring 300 more. Most of the casualties, including 88 of the dead, were Australian tourists. • Al-Qaeda claimed responsibility.
Madrid Trains March 11, 2004	• A series of coordinated bombings of a commuter train system killed 192 and wounded 2,050. • Al-Qaeda claimed responsibility, stating the attacks were revenge for Spain's collaboration with U.S. President Bush and his allies. There is some evidence, however, suggesting the bombers did not have ties to al-Qaeda, and the group simply took "advantage" of the situation.
London Subway July 7, 2005	• A coordinated series of bombs struck the city's public transportation system during the morning rush hour. Fifty-two people were killed, including the alleged bombers. Approximately 700 were injured. • Al-Qaeda claimed responsibility.

These attacks and their geographical distribution reflect the goals articulated by bin Laden's *fatwa* regarding the U.S., the West, and secular Arab regimes that have allowed the *infidel* to violate the purity of Arab lands.

> The ruling to kill the Americans and their allies — civilians and military — is an individual duty for every Muslim who can do it in any country in which it is possible to do it, in order to liberate the al-Aqsa Mosque and the holy mosque [Mecca] from their grip, and in order for their armies to move out of all the lands of Islam, defeated and unable to threaten any Muslim. This is in accordance with the words of Almighty God, "and fight the pagans all together as they fight you all together," and "fight them until there is no more tumult or oppression, and there prevail justice and faith in God."[3]

The scope of the organization's operational capability — both *how* and *where* — reflects implementation of the *fatwa*. In analyzing geopolitics and terrorism, al-Qaeda represents the internationalization of terrorism.[4] However, not all attacks are conducted directly by al-Qaeda. Rather, the influence of bin Laden as inspirational leader has led to the creation of "bin Laden and projeny" as local "franchise" terror organizations carry out attacks in the *spirit* of al-Qaeda, but not in the name of al-Qaeda.

Bin Laden's personal wealth provides the organization freedom from state sponsorship — and therefore pressure. While bin Laden is dependent on states (in the past Sudan, most recently Afghanistan, presently perhaps Pakistan) for physical haven, the organization has largely been able to establish an independent enclave within the supporting state devoid of financial dependence. Because financial resources are not an issue, bin Laden need not do any state's bidding. Contrast this to the PLO, which, while independent, could be viewed as having been part of a larger structure. Al-Qaeda *is itself the larger structure.*

1. Franchises — Homegrown Terrorism

The bombing of the Madrid train station and the London subway bombings marked a dramatic development in terrorism. Unlike the 9/11 attacks — al-Qaeda operatives specifically sent to the U.S. — both

---

3. Osama bin Laden, Second Fatwa, originally published on February 23, 1998. Full text available at http://www.pbs.org/newshour/terrorism/international/fatwa_1998.html/.

4. Al-Qaeda is an international organization founded in 1988 by veterans of the Soviet War in Afghanistan. The group made up exclusively of Sunni Muslims. The ideology of the group is influenced by Islamic author Sayyid Qutb. One of his most lasting ideas is that some Muslims are apostates — including leaders of Muslim countries who failed to enforce sharia law. Al-Qaeda members have also promoted the idea that Shi'ites are heretics. It has been labled a terrorist organization by the UN Security Council, NATO, the Commission of the European Communities of the European Union, the U.S. Department of State, among others.

the Madrid and London bombings were committed by individuals living in Spain and England prior to their involvement with terrorism. In the case of the London bombings, Mohammed Sidique Khan lived in Dewsbury, England with his pregnant wife and child; Shehzad Tanweer lived in Leeds with his parents; Germaine Lindsay lived in Aylesbury withh his pregnant wife; and Hasib Hussain lived in Leeds with his brother and sister-in-law. In Madrid, a loose group of Morrocan, Syrian, and Algerian Muslims inspired by (though not directly connected with) al-Qaeda carried out the attacks.

From a geopolitical perspective the distinction is enormous; a previously external-only threat has become internal. While expressions such as "a fifth column" and "the threat from within" are replete with negative political connotation, the increasing domestication of al-Qaeda is undeniable. Though some actors are akin to "keystone cops" (including the Miami-based indivduals who intended to blow up the Chicago Sears Tower, but did not possess the means, resources, or technical ability to actually do so), the intention and planning of others makes it clear that al-Qaeda franchising is a geopolitical reality. Were bin Laden to be killed, the significance would be minimal. President Bush's cowboy-like statement referring to bin Laden in the aftermath of 9/11 — "I want 'em dead or alive" — was inappropriate then, irrelevant today.

2. Preventing Homegrown Terrorism

What can be done to stop homegrown terrorists? Clearly, law enforcement officials need powers to stop attacks before they are committed. This suggests serious discussion devoid of the "twenty-second sound-bite" culture that defines current American political discourse regarding issues such as the efficacy and legality of the PATRIOT Act's oft-maligned business records provision, referred to by critics as the "library records" provision. This provision provides investigators access to records voluntarily left in the hands of third parties.

As an example, if a homegrown terrorist in the U.S. buys components necessary to build a bomb similar to those used in London, access to the records of such a purchase are critical. There is no protected privacy right in information that individuals voluntarily leave with third parties. National security cannot rest on whether a store clerk understands an individual is purchasing bomb components — especially considering that the clerk may know the individual personally and have no reason to suspect him or her.

Furthermore, sophisticated risk assessment models must be developed that include the prototyping of potential suicide bombers. As the suicide bomber may well be homegrown, the intelligence gathering must be expanded to include a new population group—individuals living in our midst.

Risk assessment carries a political cost—projects previously funded by Congress may no longer warrant funding. Regions and sites previously considered susceptible to attack may be determined to be a low priority for terrorists. Cost-benefit analysis must be become more than a buzz-word, and the responses to homegrown terrorism need to adapt as readily as this new threat is capable of adapting.

Difference Between Hamas, al-Qaeda, and the "Franchises"

GEOGRAPHIC-SPECIFIC: HAMAS	INTERNATIONAL: AL-QAEDA	HYBRID: "FRANCHISES"
Single-issue organization seeking the establishment of a religious state; avoids outside influences. George Washington's famous warning at his Farewell Address regarding the dangers of "foreign entanglements" is relevant to how Hamas operates.	Seeks global jihad implemented at three primary targets.	Influenced by the teachings of bin Laden and other leaders, but not operating in concert with nor on especially on the behalf of al-Qaeda. Unlike geographic-specific organizations like Hamas, these local groups do not have local goals such as the establishment of an independent state. Rather, while their targets are local, their goals are international, making them more akin to groups like al-Qaeda.

Homegrown terrorism that intends to effect political change (with-drawal of Spanish forces from Iraq) or to attack symbols (Fort Dix, London train bombings) in accordance with al-Qaeda principles is significantly different from geographic-specific terrorism intended to establish a state. Neither those responsible for the attacks in Madrid nor London intended to create a new state—while their acts of terrorism are intended to strike at geographic-specific targets (England, Spain), their end game is funda-mentally different from that of Hamas. In that sense, the "franchisee" goals are more in accordance with al-Qaeda than with Hamas. That is the case even though both the franchisee and Hamas actors are home-grown rather than externally based. From the perspective of global *jihad*, al-Qaeda represents a dual manifestation of the challenge facing the West and Arab regimes.

QUESTIONS TO CONSIDER

1. What do the franchises mean from a geopolitical perspective?
2. How does this affect operational counterterrorism?
3. What is the significance as states determine how to respond legally to terrorism?
4. How does this discussion affect the definition of terrorism and the motivations of terrorists?

How states respond to various threats (immediate and distant, direct and indirect) determines domestic, military, and foreign policies. However, as unilateralism has proven largely ineffective, state policy does not take place in a vacuum. Accordingly, external and internal factors alike influence counterterrorism measures national leaders must implement. Should states apply different counterterroism measures for each of the three forms of terrorism discussed above?

In responding to Hamas terrorism, Israel focuses solely on the organization's operatives, primarily (but not exclusively) in the Gaza Strip. As Israel does not distinguish between what Hamas defines as operational and political leaders, all Hamas members actively involved in the organization are considered legitimate targets. However, Hamas is not an international terrorism organization nor do its members use foreign countries as their base of operations. Israel's operational counterterrorism aimed at Hamas is limited to a very specific location. In responding to homegrown terrorism, the U.S., England, and Spain need to determine the following:

- Will they respond? Spain's sole response to the train bombing was to withdraw from Iraq, in accordance with the election eve promise Prime Minister Jose Luis Rodriguez Zapatero gave; the U.S. has responded to planned attacks such as Fort Dix by arresting involved individuals but has not acted operationally; England drafted new legislation intended to severely limit civil and political rights.
- What are the limits of response?
- What civil and political rights can be "waived" in response to homegrown terrorism?
- Does homegrown terrorism linked to international terrorism significantly differ from homegrown terrorism without international links?

These questions are perhaps best answered today not by examining how these nations respond to purely homegrown or international terrorism, but to what is a more complicated paradigm — Iraq.

D. WHEN LOCAL AND INTERNATIONAL TERRORISM MIX

Discussing counterterrorism and Iraq in the same sentence is tricky because it seems to make the assumption that there was a connection between 9/11 and Saddam Hussein. This section is written under the premise that the Bush Administration's efforts to link the two was — to be blunt — a fallacy, if not worse. That fallacy and its enormous fallout has led directly to the loss of thousands of American lives. It has been described as a fiasco. If there was no link between 9/11 and Saddam Hussein, how is it relevant to the question at hand?

In the context of geopolitics and terrorism, Iraq is the most important contemporary arena we can examine. It involves long-term strategic implications that will determine American counterterrorism, foreign policy, and military strategy for years to come. However, as our focus is terrorism, the other two issues will not be directly discussed (though their impact and relevance will be indirectly addressed).

In determining which of three previously discussed paradigms most closely resembles the current Iraqi paradigm, I suggest that the proper point of reference is Afghanistan of the late 1970s-1980s. The geopolitical significance of that paradigm in the context of terrorism and counterterrorism is extraordinary. As recounted in great detail elsewhere (for example, Steve Coll's *Ghost Wars*),[5] the 1979 Soviet Union invasion into Afghanistan provided bin Laden with an opportunity to both engage a nation's (Soviet Union) military in conflict and develop organizational abilities. The ultimate withdrawal of Soviet forces from Afghanistan is a defining moment in al-Qaeda's history and a signature event in understanding bin Laden's extraordinary stature in the Arab world (unrelated to 9/11).

What, then, is Iraq? Though Saddam Hussein and his regime have been relegated to the history pages, American forces are the daily targets of Improvised Explosive Devices (IED) attacks. Otherwise known as "roadside bombs," IEDs are a particularly problematic form of terror bombing. Activated in a variety of manners, from trip-wire to a soldier's step, the effects are devastating.

---

5. Steve Coll, Ghost Wars (2004).

The threat of IED's—worldwide and specifically in Iraq—continues to grow. A number of high-level commissions have held hearings, conducted research and invested resources in an effort to develop a satisfactory response. To date, the U.S. has been unable to provide U.S. troops with an effective solution.

From the terrorist perspective, the IED is a low-risk, high-payoff enterprise. The probability is very low that the individual responsible for triggering the IED will be identified after the attack. The only way to positively identify individuals responsible for IED attacks is at the moment when they are transporting and detonating the devices.

In its simplest form, an IED is an easy-to-make, often homemade device that can cause enormous damage. IED's fall into two categories: (1) package-type and (2) vehicle-borne. With limited technical knowledge and easily accessible materials, a terrorist can cause a massive detonation, shredding personnel and vehicles. Terrorists do not have the ability to meet conventional armed forces directly, so the IED is their preferred tactic. A device capable of inflicting considerable damage can be detonated with the terrorists nowhere to be found. Most IEDs encountered by coalition troops in Iraq are remotely detonated by cordless phones or car alarm remotes.

In Iraq, IEDs have resulted in 1,447 U.S. military fatalities as of August 1, 2007—or 39.5 percent of all fatalities. Clearly, they play an important role in the current conflict in Iraq.

There are risks inherent in such an indiscriminate weapon. Killing innocent civilians reduces the credibility of insurgents and increases the risks that the local population will turn against them. Therefore, some insurgents give warnings to the local population, either by word of mouth or by employing marking systems (a line of broken glass on road, empty rice sacks tied to light posts, a pile of rocks) to indicate that an IED has been placed in the area. Intelligence sources report that insurgents will tell local shop owners not to come to work on a particular day, or instruct the local populace to avoid a specific intersection. These subtle indicators can be detected if forces on the ground are trained to look for them or if surveillance operations are conducted.

The daily threat posed by the IEDs to coalition forces in Iraq is akin to the daily terrorism threat presented by Hamas suicide bombers to the Israeli population. However, unlike the geographic-specific, single-issue focus of Hamas, the groups attacking American forces are unitary neither in their origin nor in their goals. The American invasion of Iraq has resulted in the infiltration—if not creation—of a polyglot of terrorist organizations. In addition to fighting American forces, the terrorist organizations are also engaged in battle with each other.

QUESTIONS TO CONSIDER

1. What are the geopolitical considerations in the context of terrorism that the U.S. faces?
2. How is a viable operational counterterrorism policy to be developed given multiple threats and multiple forces?
3. What are the geopolitical ramifications of multiple terror organizations?
4. Can a clear policy be realistically developed in such a paradigm?
5. Are American forces in Iraq at an advantage or disadvantage?
6. Is an IED in Iraq an inherent aspect of the larger conflict?
7. Why is al-Qaeda in Iraq?
8. What are the goals of the various groups fighting in Iraq?
9. Is Iraq embroiled in a civil war between Shiites, Sunnis, and Kurds? If so, what other groups or interests are at play?

Are American forces facing an insurgency, guerilla warfare, terrorism — or something new, such as a "hybrid paradigm?" In the aftermath of the fall of Saddam Hussein, U.S. forces are not engaged in traditional warfare against a regular army. However, in seeking to understand the geopolitical significance of al-Qaeda's actions in Iraq, the question is whether the scenario differs significantly from what Israel faces from Hamas, what England faces with respect to homegrown terrorism, or what American targets encounter in the context of global jihad.

Much like the discussion in Chapter 2 regarding the multiple motivations that drive terrorists, the answer with respect to how to define the conflict in Iraq is not black-and-white. There is clearly sectarian conflict (Shiites and Sunnis) as well as civil war (Shiites, Sunnis and Kurds) and aspects of jihadism (al-Qaeda forces attacking the U.S.). The Hamas-like, single issue, geographic-specific terrorism model is inapplicable to al-Qaeda in Iraq. With respect to homegrown terrorism, though Iraqis have joined al-Qaeda, the forces that attack American forces are outside-driven. That is dissimilar from the homegrown terrorism model that the U.S., Spain, and England have encountered in the past few years.

Is Iraq, then, part of the larger global jihadism similar in nature to 9/11? Is Iraq like a daily version of the Khobar Towers or U.S.S. Cole — attacks against American targets outside the U.S. in a continued effort to "cleanse" Arab lands of the *infidel*, as directed by bin Laden's *fatwa*?

If terrorism is indeed "cause" related, then it would seem that American forces are subjected to terrorism — the cause being the driving of America out of another Arab land. However, if terrorism attacks are intended to intimidate a civilian population, then the picture is less clear-cut. The daily targets of al-Qaeda attacks are American forces rather than the Iraqi population. That being said, the havoc wreaked on the Iraqi population is an undeniable tragedy.

From a geopolitical perspective, Iraq presents multiple conflicts in which various groups (secular and religious) seek to advance their different goals. With respect to al-Qaeda, the organization's primary aims appear to be two-fold: to drive American forces out of Iraq and to maximize the opportunity the U.S. has presented with respect to recruiting and providing "on the job training." From a geopolitical perspective, U.S. decision makers need to determine what price will be paid for withdrawal from Iraq and whether the cost is justified.

Multiple perspectives must be considered for the cost: loss of life, resource allocation, the fading support of the Iraqi people for the American presence, and serious questions regarding the ability of the U.S. military to successfully engage determined terrorists in conflict. With respect to price, the overriding question is whether withdrawal would be perceived as weakness by Iran as it "goes nuclear."

To come full circle—al-Qaeda in Iraq is a combination of two paradigms: homegrown and global jihadist terrorism. It bears little, if any, resemblance to Hamas-like terrorism. The geopolitical ramifications of American policy in Iraq have consequences that extend beyond the three additional paradigms discussed in this chapter. Because of its complexity—defined as the number of conflicts occurring simultaneously and high casualty count among combatants and non-combatants alike—this fourth paradigm undoubtedly presents the most complicated (and therefore fraught with danger) challenge to policy and decision makers alike attempting to understand geopolitics and terrorism.

We have presented four relevant paradigms: region-specific, international, homegrown, and a hybrid of homegrown and international. In analyzing geopolitics and terrorism, it is incumbent upon decision makers to determine terrorist motivations and to carefully place these motivations within an accurate geopolitical context.

If, in the past, geopolitics focused solely on the balance of power among nation-states, the multiple paradigms of the contemporary age present enormous challenges to decision makers. The traditional "balancing power" analysis has been replaced by a model comprised of numerous, distinct threats emanating from different sources.

CHAPTER 4

THE LIMITS OF POWER AND OPERATIONAL COUNTERTERRORISM

A. INTRODUCTION

There is no such thing as perfection in operational counterterrorism. State action aimed at legitimate targets will inevitably affect innocent civilians ("collateral damage") who are non-combatants that should be protected. A legitimate target is an individual who is involved in acts of terrorism against the state and is subject to relevant state action.[1] The question is how a state can conduct its counterterrorism policies in a manner that effectively addresses terrorism while minimizing injury—physical, economic, social, etc.—to civilians.

Aharon Barak, former President of the Supreme Court of Israel, has written that the state must adopt a policy of "self-imposed restraints" when determining the limits of power. While commanders in Israel found this philosophy highly problematic—if not unreasonable—operational counterterrorism must be guided by restraints. Otherwise, the indiscriminate killing of innocent civilians is all but guaranteed. Yet from the perspective of decision makers and commanders, "limits of power" suggest that those who endanger the state, its citizens, and its assets will somehow benefit because the state will not maximize its operational capability. The limits of power reflect an asymmetrical conflict—one side fights to the fullest of its ability, the other voluntarily limits its actions. In the opinions of some, this means that operational counterterrorism may well favor terrorists. Put bluntly: If the state limits its responses to protect innocent civilians, do terrorists enjoy a degree of immunity?

---

1. See Chapter 5 for a full discussion of open fire orders.

Terrorists benefit from the element of surprise in choosing when to attack, while states acting in accordance with the rule of law and morality in armed conflict limit their operational response. A full-scale response would not only violate international law, but result in significant "blowback"—a term of art for the escalation of violence that can be inadvertently triggered by government response. If state forces kill a terrorist suspect, the relevant terrorist organization may conduct a suicide bombing, killing numerous innocent civilians. If a child witnesses his or her parents humiliated at military checkpoints, the child may grow up to sympathize with terror organizations, if not join them outright. Yet the state cannot be forced into inaction for fear of unknown negative consequences. Therefore, the state must constantly evaluate its actions to determine whether they are in accordance with international law.

B. LIMITING COLLATERAL DAMAGE

The following table examines the four international law principles relevant to this discussion.

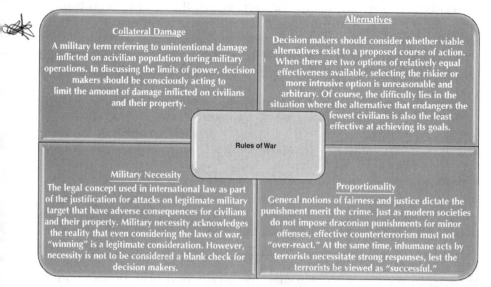

Collateral Damage	Alternatives
A military term referring to unintentional damage inflicted on acivilian population during military operations. In discussing the limits of power, decision makers should be consciously acting to limit the amount of damage inflicted on civilians and their property.	Decision makers should consider whether viable alternatives exist to a proposed course of action. When there are two options of relatively equal effectiveness available, selecting the riskier or more intrusive option is unreasonable and arbitrary. Of course, the difficulty lies in the situation where the alternative that endangers the fewest civilians is also the least effective at achieving its goals.

Rules of War

Military Necessity	Proportionality
The legal concept used in international law as part of the justification for attacks on legitimate military target that have adverse consequences for civilians and their property. Military necessity acknowledges the reality that even considering the laws of war, "winning" is a legitimate consideration. However, necessity is not to be considered a blank check for decision makers.	General notions of fairness and justice dictate the punishment merit the crime. Just as modern societies do not impose draconian punishments for minor offenses, effective counterterrorism must not "over-react." At the same time, inhumane acts by terrorists necessitate strong responses, lest the terrorists be viewed as "successful."

Understanding these four principles is essential to appreciating the limits of power. The fundamental purpose of these principles is to strike a balance between the state's legitimate national security interests and its obligation to minimize harm to innocent civilians.

In the counterterrorism paradigm, as opposed to the war paradigm, this balance presents an extraordinary challenge to military commanders. In traditional war, soldiers were readily identifiable by their insignia and uniforms, carried their arms openly, were obliged to conduct themselves in accordance with the laws of war, and were part of a command structure. The terrorist paradigm is quite the opposite. Therefore, not only is it difficult to strike the balance between national security and protecting civilians — it is difficult to tell the difference between targets and civilians.

Example 1

An IDF battalion commander[2] is ordered to detain three suspected terrorists deemed to be threats to state security. According to the operational plan, the mission is to be carried out mid-morning on a weekday, specifically minimizing the presence of school children in the streets. The available intelligence suggests the three targets are hiding in the vicinity of the town square.

As the commander and his forces approach the city, it is brought to his attention that hundreds of school children are milling about the town square. A quick check indicates that the reason is neither an Islamic holiday nor a remembrance day for a dead local leader. Rather, spotters from the terrorist organization had noticed the IDF force approaching the city, and terrorist leaders had ordered principals to immediately close schools so that the school children would act as human shields for the terrorists.

The result: Hundreds of children released early from school are wandering around the targeted area.

The commander's dilemma: To continue with the operation, thereby *potentially* risking the children's lives; to abort the mission; to play "cat and mouse" in hopes that the soldiers will eventually be able to identify the targets among the children, though the end result will likely still be aborting the mission, leaving the children and the terrorists unharmed.

The commander's decision: To abort the operation.

The commander's rationale: Entering the village square under the circumstances as they had developed would have, *in all probability*, either led to injury or death of numerous children and/or significantly reduced the opportunity to detain the three suspects.

As a final note, the three suspects were subsequently detained in another operation.

---

2. This vignette is based on a private conversation I had with the battalion commander in a professional context.

In addressing the limits of power, it is critical to understand that field commanders are responsible for operational counterterrorism decisions. The manner in which commanders — junior and senior — make decisions is the essence of operational counterterrorism. It is also the ultimate application of the limits of power. High-ranking decision makers can implement all the policies in the world, but the boots on the ground generally implement them.

The following represents an alternate — and tragic — example of when a field commander makes the wrong decision. While not directly related to counterterrorism, the fact pattern and consequences are highly relevant to our discussion regarding the limits of power.

EXAMPLE 2

On the eve of the 1956 Sinai Campaign (a war between Egypt and Israel limited to the Sinai Peninsula that also involved England and France), curfew was imposed on Israeli Arabs living in Israel. In a meeting involving Border Police officers charged with imposing the curfew, the commanders were asked what would be the fate of day laborers returning to their homes from the fields who were unaware of the curfew order.

The commander's response: Allah yerachmun — Arabic for "God have mercy on them."

The result: The killing of 48 innocent men, women, and children.

The consequences: Known as the Kfar Kassem incident, the case gave birth to the phrase "black flag" in regard to blatantly illegal military orders. Eleven of those involved were charged with crimes; eight were ultimately convicted. Significant re-examination took place in Israel regarding the manner in which military units are prepared for operational missions.

What do these two very different scenarios above contribute to a discussion regarding the limits of power? In Example 1, the battalion commander chose to exercise discretion and did not execute a lawful, operational order. Example 2 not only represents the consequences of willfully obeying an unlawful order, but also illustrates the consequences of failure to understand the limits of power.

A discussion regarding the limits of power must be sensitive to the contrasting narratives at stake. In the first example, the battalion commander determined that fulfilling the order would result in the deaths of children. Yet from a terrorist — and possibly from the community's — perspective, the commander's decision may be interpreted as weakness. According to the commander, his superiors overwhelmingly supported his decision. While his peer group was largely supportive, his soldiers were divided. Those opposed to his decision not to pursue the operation thought it was a sign of command weakness; those who supported the decision viewed counterterrorism from a long-term perspective.

In the same vein, it is important for decision makers to determine whether a reflexive military response to an act of terrorism is effective. Perhaps "picking and choosing" when to respond is more effective. From a decision maker's perspective, the limits of power cannot be viewed in the abstract. They must always be determined by the factual situation at hand. While it may be easy to see the alternatives presented to a commander in hindsight, it is often very difficult to sort them out in the heat of the moment.

While the international law principles previously defined *are* absolute, as is the state's obligation to respect them, the decision whether to engage is not absolute. There was nothing to force the commander in the first example to continue with his mission, aside from his command structure. Yet the decree against collateral damage is not absolute; rather, international law only requires that states minimize collateral damage. From an operational perspective, eliminating collateral damage is all but impossible. Does this mean that the restrictions international law imposes on states are meaningless?

This issue is best analyzed as an integrative—rather than linear—paradigm. While nation-states are obligated to respect international law, the reality of operational counterterrorism is that terrorists provoke state actors—commanders and soldiers—to violate international law principles. Perhaps the most egregious example is "human shielding": the deliberate surrounding of terrorists by women and children in order to protect the terrorist. Should the commander decide to continue with the mission, at the risk of injuring or killing innocent civilians, he or she risks violating the principle of minimizing collateral damage.

We must ask what certain terms mean to a commander. What does "minimize" mean to the commander? How is he or she to determine who is an innocent civilian? Because both terms are subject to interpretation, the commanders' operational decision-making process is dependent on a variety of variables reflecting the complexity of defining the limits of power. These variables include:

- **The nature of the mission:** If the mission involves killing a particular terrorist, will there be another "window of opportunity" in the future should the commander determine that the risk to civilians is too high *at this moment*? Is the commander of the professional opinion that the mission can be accomplished with minimal injury to non-combatants? How imminent is the threat allegedly presented by the suspected terrorists?

- **The quality of the available intelligence information:** Is the commander convinced the information is sufficiently reliable to engage the terrorist, regardless of potential harm to nearby innocent civilians? Has the commander's military training emphasized international law and morality in armed conflict? Has the mission been sufficiently articulated to the commander?
- **The degree of risk to civilians:** Does the commander even know that the innocent civilians at risk are civilians? Are the "shielders" themselves members of the terrorists' organization? Can the commander trust that his/her soldiers have been adequately trained to minimize harm to civilians?
- **The "outsider's" perspective:** Will the terrorist's community view a decision not to engage as weakness? Will an action serve as a lightning rod to recruit additional terrorists? How will the civilian population view the action? The media? The international community?

Virtually all operational scenarios involve some risk to civilians and their property; there is no scenario where the chance of mistake or failure does not exist. If the nation-state were to order its forces to view the prohibition of harm to civilians as an absolute, rather than as a concept subject to interpretation, then the questions posed above would be the death knell for operational counterterrorism. Conversely, if commanders are trained—and retrained—to appreciate that the complexity of international law must be tailored to operational realities, then a balance between counterterrorism and international law is a viable reality.

In analyzing the battalion commander's decision-making process according to the questions above, there are a number of issues to consider. We must ask ourselves whether the decision to emphasize the limits of power is operationally effective and realistic. Does the state lose its deterrent ability with respect to future acts of terrorism by respecting international law and imposing limits on its power? A discussion about the limits of power must be subjected to practical judgment.

C. HOW TO TREAT TERRORIST SUSPECTS

Is terrorism an act of war, a crime, or something else? Answering this question is necessary to determine how suspects should be handled prior to engagement and how detainees should be treated after capture. After all, a situation where a police officer is empowered to open fire at a suspected criminal is rare indeed—essentially limited to scenarios where the officer was in mortal fear of his or her life, or where the life of a bystander was immediately threatened. In contrast, a soldier can generally engage an enemy soldier in all but a few circumstances. The fact that the soldiers are engaged in war dictates the rules by which they both abide. Therefore, it is clear that the limits of state power in a criminal context are far more constrictive than in a warfare context. So where are the limits in a terrorism context?

In Example 1 (see page 67), the three wanted terrorists were to be captured in accordance with a lawful order. In the terrorism paradigm, individuals suspected of terrorism are sometimes detained in the field after engaging the state force. Such a scenario presents a clear case to commanders because they can be relatively certain that the individual in question is a legitimate target. Yet terrorist suspects can also be detained at home, work, school, or church when the individual is not actively involved in an act of terrorism, but available intelligence suggests he either has in the past or will in the future.

In such a case, should the individual be treated as an enemy soldier or a criminal suspect? Or something else entirely? In liberal democracies, the detained individual is guaranteed rights and protections. One of the most important questions facing democracies is articulating what rights to grant detainees. That question is critical to the question this chapter addresses — the limits of powers.

It seems clear that terrorist suspects are neither criminals as understood in the criminal law paradigm, nor are they prisoners of war (POWs). But then what are they? Various terms have been suggested, including enemy combatant, illegal combatant, illegal belligerent, and enemy belligerent.

All these definitions have failed to provide clear answers as to how the state should limit its power in response to these individuals — yet all start at the same logical premise. All individuals have rights, but those rights can be limited given certain factual circumstances. Therefore, to determine how much the state can limit the individual suspect's rights, we must define the conflict itself. Is this a war? Is this a "war on terrorism"? Is this a "police action"?

Different societies answer this question in different ways, if at all. The United States in particular has failed to answer this question with specificity. In numerous decisions (*Rasul v. Bush*,[3] *Rumsfeld v. Padilla*,[4] *Hamdan v. Rumsfeld*,[5] *Hamdi v. Rumsfeld*[6]), the U.S. Supreme Court has failed to articulate what rights to grant the suspected terrorists. Similarly, Congress has failed in its constitutionally granted oversight powers. The executive has

---

3. Rasul v. Bush, 542 U.S. 466 (2004).
4. Rumsfeld v. Padilla, 542 U.S. 426 (2004).
5. Hamdan v. Rumsfeld, 548 U.S. 557 (2006).
6. Hamdi v. Rumsfeld, 542 U.S. 507 (2004).

called this a "war on terror" and provided post-9/11 detainees with fewer rights than POWs.

The term adopted by the Israel Supreme Court—"armed conflict short of war"—reflects that the conflict is not a classic war (which according to international law can only be conducted between states) and also does not fall within the traditional criminal law paradigm. This view reflects a "hybrid" view, which adopts aspects of both the POW and criminal law paradigms.

D. THE HYBRID PARADIGM

The hybrid paradigm is philosophically and jurisprudentially founded on the principle that the accused must be brought to some form of trial, but that the American criminal law process is inapplicable to the current conflict. Accordingly, in order to guarantee the suspect *certain* rights and privileges, the hybrid paradigm is predicated on the following: the use of intelligence, torture-less interrogations, the right to appeal to an independent judiciary, the right to counsel of the suspect's own choosing, known terms of imprisonment, and procedures to prevent indefinite detention.

Analysis regarding the limits of power must extend beyond detention in the field. The legal process in its entirety must meet constitutional muster and international law standards. The concept of self-imposed restraints must be applied uniformly to all aspects of operational counterterrorism; the state cannot pick and chose what aspects of the law it respects.

In analyzing the rule of law — and therefore the limits of power — it is critical to discuss what are the state's goals. The discussion must focus on a number of different considerations and variables:

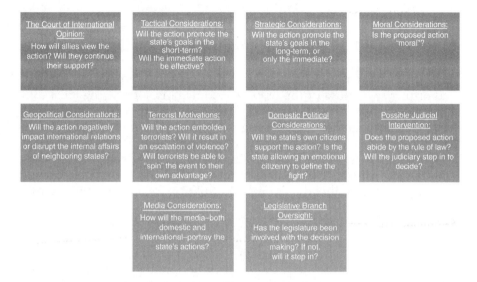

The Court of International Opinion: How will allies view the action? Will they continue their support?	Tactical Considerations: Will the action promote the state's goals in the short-term? Will the immediate action be effective?	Strategic Considerations: Will the action promote the state's goals in the long-term, or only the immediate?	Moral Considerations: Is the proposed action "moral"?
Geopolitical Considerations: Will the action negatively impact international relations or disrupt the internal affairs of neighboring states?	Terrorist Motivations: Will the action embolden terrorists? Will it result in an escalation of violence? Will terrorists be able to "spin" the event to their own advantage?	Domestic Political Considerations: Will the state's own citizens support the action? Is the state allowing an emotional citizenry to define the fight?	Possible Judicial Intervention: Does the proposed action abide by the rule of law? Will the judiciary step in to decide?
Media Considerations: How will the media–both domestic and international–portray the state's actions?	Legislative Branch Oversight: Has the legislature been involved with the decision making? If not, will it step in?		

States that adhere to the principles of the rule of law obligate themselves to respecting the rights of the individual. Determining which of these rights are absolute is paramount. The traditional battlefield where large armies once fought has been replaced by the "zone of conflict." The zone of conflict is not a static geographic region, but a fluid concept reflecting the reality of operational counterterrorism. Preserving those rights in all the relevant arenas, ranging from the actual operational engagement to the interrogation setting to the courtroom is critical to the limits of power.

For example, an initial lawful detention is as important to this process as a lawful arrest is to the criminal process. A lawful detention process in the terrorism paradigm must be premised either on (a) reliable and corroborated intelligence or (b) the individual's specific actions against soldiers or civilians. If a detention is not based on this "probable cause for terrorism," every step in the process afterward will be tainted. The unintended consequences of such violations may include the detainee's release from detention. This means that the hybrid paradigm (rather than the terrorism paradigm presently articulated by the Bush Administration), will result in suspects being released if the state does not adhere to legal limits.

The factors involved in analyzing whether — and why — the rule of law is respected extends beyond the law exclusively. Because of the emergence of what the American military refers to as the "strategic corporal" — the constant presence of the media in the zone of conflict ensuring that violations of human rights are immediately viewed worldwide — the relationship between the rule of law and counterterrorism is even more critical than that between the rule of law and traditional warfare.

E. HOW DO SOLDIERS KNOW HOW TO ACT?

In planning operational counterterrorism measures, commanders are limited primarily because of the presence of civilians. One of the most difficult issues in operational counterterrorism is defining who is a legitimate target and subsequently identifying *that* individual in the "zone of combat." The amount of time the soldier or commander has to decide *who* is a legitimate target is less than the time required to read this sentence. The stakes are also higher — kill the innocent civilian, and there is literally hell to pay. Decide incorrectly, and the soldier, in all probability, dies.

EXAMPLE 3

> I had command responsibility for the development of an IDF interactive training video that taught soldiers and junior commanders how to conduct themselves among a civilian population during armed conflict. One of the primary principles the video stressed was the obligation by soldiers to respect the religious symbols/artifacts of the civilian population. I demonstrated the video to numerous units, including an infantry battalion.
>
> Later, some of these soldiers were approached at a checkpoint by a Palestinian with a prayer rug. The soldiers chose to not ask him to unfurl the rug; inside was an AK-47. Both soldiers died when the man opened fire at close range.

How does the soldier determine who is a legitimate target? A legitimate target is an individual who presents life-threatening danger to the soldier, the soldier's unit, and/or innocent civilians. Legitimate targets include men, women, and minors alike. Clearly, the identification of a child as a threat is problematic — but children *are* committing suicide bombings. Whether they do so on their own volition or as the result of tragic family or community pressures is irrelevant from the perspective of a soldier facing potential attack. The TNT about to explode is affected neither by the age nor gender of the individual pressing the lever of the suicide belt.

Even if an individual is identified, how do soldiers know if they are facing life threatening danger? What does "life threatening danger" mean in the context of operational counterterrorism? Consider the following scenarios.

EXAMPLE 4

The soldier is facing a crowd of people, some of whom are throwing Molotov cocktails. Among those *not* throwing the cocktails are innocent bystanders, as well as potential instigators who may have been clever enough to not throw anything themselves.

The soldier is facing gunfire coming from a particular alley or rooftop where a number of individuals are present, perhaps including the source of the gunfire.

While legal advisors can prepare criteria and checklists pertaining to the rules of engagement (see Chapter 5), the ultimate decision is largely predicated on the individual soldier's instinct. While commanders have enormous influence regarding soldier conduct, both by personal example (the battalion commander in Example 1 represents one side of the coin; the commander at Kfar Kassem in Example 2 the flip side) and training, the final decision whether to engage a target oftentimes rests with the soldier.

The limits of power, accordingly, are ultimately determined at the most basic of levels. The battalion commander in the first example, in choosing to abort the mission, was signaling to multiple audiences that unless the target is extraordinarily dangerous and presents an immediate threat, the "another day" theory was appropriate. Yet it is possible that the decision to not go forth *was* a sign of weakness in the face of sustained and consistent Palestinian terrorism.

Conversely, the Border Police commander from the second example reflects indiscriminate decision-making. The actors in that scenario did not bother distinguishing between legitimate and illegitimate targets. The subsequent actions of the field commander who actually gave the "open fire" orders is but a continuation of the fateful words "God be with them," with one critical distinction. The field commander saw the innocent men, women, and children; he saw his victims.

EXAMPLE 5

In the aftermath of a Passover eve attack that killed 28 Israelis, the IDF forcefully entered major cities in the West Bank. According to reliable intelligence information, parts of the Jenin refugee camp had been turned into an arms cache of significant proportions. Then-IDF Chief of Staff Shaul Mofaz ordered a reserve infantry unit to enter the refugee camp in an effort to identify and destroy the cache. In the resulting operation, 13 soldiers were killed.

continued on next page

Though Mofaz was largely credited for seeking to minimize the loss of innocent Palestinian lives, a minority viewpoint suggested that the Chief of Staff should be held accountable for the deaths of the 13 soldiers. After all, Mofaz was rhetorically asked, what army knowingly sends soldiers to their deaths when an operational alternative was readily available: pinpointed aerial bombing of the camp?

The criticism suggests that respect for international law standards and the court of international opinion led Mofaz to grant ascendancy to the limits of power rather than perform his primary duty: protect the lives of IDF soldiers.

Balancing a nation's primary obligation—to protect its own citizens—can paradoxically find itself at odds with other obligations such as upholding the standards of international law and observing the limits of power. Though counterterrorism seeks to protect the state's citizens, it can also lead to the deaths of innocent civilians. Losing soldiers, such as in Example 5 above, creates an atmosphere in which the balancing becomes even more difficult. Field conditions, operational realities, and tensions affect soldiers' conduct (soldiers are impacted by the deaths of their friends).

Again, the question is to what extent should the state engage in self-limitation. In three of the examples proposed in this chapter, different approaches with drastically different results were observed.

EXAMPLE NO. 1: TOWN SQUARE	EXAMPLE NO. 2: KFAR KASSEM	EXAMPLE NO. 5: JENIN REFUGEE CAMP
Illustrates ultimate discretion on the part of the commander. From the perspective of command influence, his decision was intended (consciously or unconsciously) to instill in his solders the "another day" theory and that operational counter-terrorism is not a "black/white" endeavor.	Illustrates total disregard for the limits of power on the part of commanders and absolute obedience to an order by the soldiers as they failed to exercise discretion.	Like Example 1, shows great respect for the limits of power and saved the lives of countless Palestinian residents of the camp.

continued on next page

EXAMPLE NO. 1: TOWN SQUARE	EXAMPLE NO. 2: KFAR KASSEM	EXAMPLE NO. 5: JENIN REFUGEE CAMP
Possibly results in emboldening terrorists.	Results in the deaths of innocent civilians and creates countless institutional problems for the Israeli military and government.	Results in the deaths of 13 Israeli soldiers. The question is whether Mofaz's decision reflects an imbalance with respect to the limits of power—it could be argued that by choosing a course of action that was more dangerous for the soldiers, the Chief of Staff was valuing Palestinian lives over the lives of the soldiers.

F. THE CONSEQUENCES OF VIOLATING THE LIMITS OF POWER

The impact of visual documentation is difficult to counter. Since after-action reports (written or verbal) are no match for the visual, whether the photo or video in question accurately depicts an event is largely insignificant.

In September 2000, a camera crew filmed a gun battle between IDF soldiers and Palestinian policemen in the Gaza Strip. Caught in the cross-fire was a small child, Muhammad Dura, whose father was desperately—and unsuccessfully—trying to shield his son from the hail of bullets.

The picture of a father embracing his young, helpless son is exponentially more powerful than any explanation various IDF officers could offer. Commissions of inquiry have examined this event; their findings have been deemed inconclusive as to whether this particular IDF unit was acting appropriately. What is clear is that the vivid picture of Muhammad Dura and his father remains in the collective memory with many long-term ramifications. The picture was effectively used as a recruiting poster by Palestinian terrorists, the IDF was depicted as a child-killing army, and Israel's military leadership was forced to spend significant time explaining the unit's actions, rather than focusing on Israel's operational needs.

A military unit that is not sensitive to humanity is operationally inferior to a unit trained to respect the limits of power. A unit that is ill-prepared to deal with the limits of power in a terrorism setting will inevitably create unintended negative consequences. Commanders can be distracted due to concerns that violations may occur and because valuable training time is lost.

G. CONCLUSION

In the previous three chapters, we discussed the definition of terrorism, terrorist motivation, and the geopolitics of terrorism. The question addressed in this chapter—how the limits of power affect operational counterterrorism—is the logical next step because actual events in the field significantly impact the tone, tenor, and results of abstract theories.

It is important to note that while this discussion can be conducted in the rarified air of academia for commanders on the ground this is the essence of command and conflict. There are no easy answers because the intangibles are no less important than articulated criteria and measurable variables. While militaries need to institutionalize field decisions to the greatest extent possible, the ultimate decision is largely predicated on the commanders' experience, training, instinct, and intuition.

The reason is clear: the commanders are the boots on the ground and their eyes see the lay of the land. While modern technology provides the commander with additional eyes and ears, he or she is the one looking into the crowd, seeking to determine who is the legitimate target—and just as importantly—who is not. What is important is whether the operational code that has been instilled in the commander stresses "active self-defense" or "limits of power."

It is also clear that there are no easy answers to these issues. The three paradigms—war, counterterrorism, and hybrid—illustrated in this chapter are meant to serve as points of discussion highlighting the complexity of the balancing act that nations must perform when formulating and conducting operational counterterrorism strategies in the field.

RULES OF ENGAGEMENT

A. INTRODUCTION

Rules of engagement illustrate how the state perceives terrorism and terrorists. If the terrorist is defined as a soldier, then traditional laws of war apply. If the suspected terrorist is viewed as a criminal, then traditional police measures are relevant. But what if terrorists inhabit a nebulous middle ground, neither soldiers nor criminals? Can operational decisions be based on pre-existing rules if the suspect is something unprecedented? How should a state actor respond when confronted with an individual suspected of committing an act of terrorism?

While policy makers debate the policy aspects of counterterrorism, and lawyers define the limits of the law, soldiers and police officers must make operational on-the-ground decisions regarding suspects. The primary decisions are whether to detain an individual and if justified, when to open fire. The rules of engagement define when "open fire" orders may be given. What is critical to the soldier and police officer is that the rules be clear, unambiguous, and facilitate operational decision-making.

Commanders must be able to clearly articulate "dos and don'ts" to soldiers serving in their unit. Implementation of the rules of engagement is ultimately a command issue. Units that violate those rules cause significant damage on a variety of levels, all relevant to successfully engaging the enemy.

"Engage" is defined as any interaction between the suspect and a force acting on behalf of the state charged with keeping public peace and security. The interaction need not necessarily involve "open fire" orders and their consequences, though that may be inevitable. The consequences depend on the actions of a variety of individuals. An open fire order is given when the commander is of the opinion that state security is endangered by a particular individual and therefore shooting that individual is warranted.

The rub from both a policy and legal perspective is that the unknowns are, in all probability, more numerous than the knowns—yet the commander still has to decide whether to give the order or not. What factors into that decision? In making this determination, the commander must define both the threat and the risk.

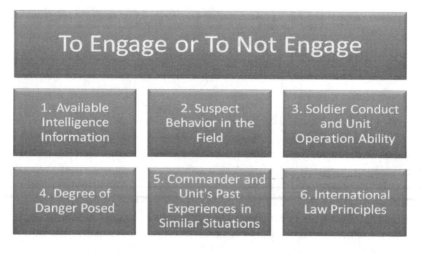

B. INTELLIGENCE INFORMATION

Intelligence is the heart and soul of operational counterterrorism. What is intelligence? It is information indicating either future activity (such as details concerning a potential terrorist attack) or suggesting who is responsible for a previous act. Intelligence alone does not justify an "open fire" order. Determining whether received intelligence is actionable depends on a four-part test: reliability, viability, validity, and corroboration.

Reliability depends on the source, but in the overwhelming majority of instances, the commander does not meet nor evaluate the source. The commander is dependent on the intelligence community's analysis of the source's trustworthiness and motives. Determining the information's reliability is one of the intelligence community's most daunting and important tasks because counterterrorism operational decisions are oftentimes predicted largely on that information.

Intelligence information largely comes from one of the following:

- **Human Intelligence (HUMINT):** Intelligence gathered from human sources — collaborators who have turned on their cell; detainees who have confessed; friendly foreign diplomats; clandestine agents; etc.

- **Signal Intelligence (SIGINT):** Intelligence gathered by interpreting communication between people or machines through the use of sophisticated electronic eavesdropping equipment.
- **Open Source Information:** Newspapers, blogs, etc.

Operational decisions should not be based *solely* on what the source has told the intelligence community. Great weight must be given both to the commander's assessment of the intelligence with respect to existing field circumstances and conditions, and the intelligence community's assessment of information received. The open fire order is given by the "boots on the ground" commander, even when the basis for the order is preexisting intelligence, precisely because the commander is present.

C. TARGETED KILLING

Targeted killing is a policy whereby an individual suspected of involvement in a serious act of terrorism is killed, provided there is no other viable alternative to prevent the attack. It is a policy practiced by the IDF, the U.S. and in the past, by the U.K. In my capacity as the Legal Advisor to the Gaza Strip Military Commander, I was involved in implementation of the policy. It is important to emphasize that an individual will only be targeted if he or she presents a serious threat to public order and safety based on criminal evidence and/or reliable, corroborated intelligence information implicating him or her with respect to a future act of terrorism. Intelligence information is considered corroborated when it is confirmed by at least two separate, unrelated sources. There also must be no reasonable alternative to the targeted killing, meaning that the international law requirement of seeking another reasonable method of incapacitating the terrorist has proved fruitless.[1]

While the decision to fire is the commander's, in an ideal situation the decision is predicated on a previously established system that has been developed to minimize risk and discretion. This process requires input from the following:

- The commander who sees the factual scenario on the ground and can address a number of issues, including whether the operational plan guarantees minimal collateral damage;
- The intelligence community who address source reliability and the nature and quality of the available information;

---

1. Robert F. Teplitz, *Taking Assassination Attempts Seriously: Did the United States Violate International Law in Forcefully Responding to the Iraqi Plot to Kill George Bush?*, 28 CORNELL INT'L L.J. 569, 610-613.

- An expert who analyzes the possible responses of the target's community;
- A legal advisor who speaks to the legality of the proposed attack, predicated on an analysis of international law, the quality of the intelligence information, and the seriousness of the terror attack the targeted individual is suspected of planning.

From the commander's perspective, once the decision to target a specific individual has been authorized, the decision to open fire depends *both* on field conditions and an absolute certainty that the targeted individual is the person in his crosshairs. While others have been involved in the authorizing process, the final decision is the commander's. To ascertain the reliability of the intelligence requires on-site verification. Once the commander is convinced that the intelligence information matches the situation on the ground, the order can be given.

This is not to suggest that mistakes do not happen. In one such operation, a significant miscalculation by structural engineers regarding the quality of the material used to construct the targeted individual's home led to its implosion. Though one individual was targeted, innocent women and children were also killed. The commander relied on expert opinion (engineers) that was clearly erroneous. Could the operator have known this? This raises an important question regarding placing limits on the commander's discretion, as he or she may not necessarily see the entire picture.

EXAMPLE

In the Gaza Strip, an IDF infantry unit had been shot at by a terrorist. By chance, an IDF helicopter was nearby. The infantry commander ordered the pilot to shoot at the individual the commander believed was responsible for shooting at the unit. The individual was seen running away from the unit.

The helicopter pilot was not convinced that the individual running was the shooter. The commander was convinced and therefore repeatedly ordered the pilot to shoot. The pilot refused to do so. After a very unpleasant exchange that escalated into mutual recriminations and threats, the pilot decided not to shoot. The individual(s) escaped unharmed.

Was he the shooter? According to the commander, yes; according to the pilot, no.

Film footage (shot from the air) showed the following: one individual shooting at the unit and another running from the unit. What seemed obvious to the commander—individual shoots then runs, was in actuality two different people. From his "on the ground" position, he could not distinguish between the two.

What is the relevance of this example? It shows that enormous care must be exercised in giving "open fire" orders. Reality is not necessarily what it is assumed to be. This is particularly the case in operational counterterrorism when terrorists and innocent civilians commingle and the risk of killing the latter outweighs the benefit of killing the former.

Accordingly, strict standards for rules of engagement are an absolute necessity. The commander, rather than the intelligence officer, must have the final say, but he or she is obligated to consider all possibilities.

1. Target's Behavior

Much like police officers in the traditional criminal law paradigm, the actions of the individual are critical. What has the person done to be deemed a threat? Why does the commander believe the individual poses a risk to the lives either of civilians or the soldiers under his or her command? Does the individual understand that the commander views him as a potential threat and that his life is at stake unless he changes his behavior?

The answers to these questions are based on subjective and objective tests alike. Let us begin with the most clear-cut scenario: the individual points a weapon in the soldiers' direction, thereby endangering them. The rules of engagement are clear: an open fire order with the intention of killing the individual would be justified. An order to wound the individual would not necessarily neutralize the threat presented by a drawn weapon.

However, if the individual makes a movement reaching for what the soldier believes to be a weapon, what do the rules of engagement allow? This is a less objective test. The soldier *assumes* the motion is for the purpose of reaching for a weapon. However, there is a possibility the individual was reaching for a document he *assumes* the soldier will request to see.

Suspect points a gun at the soldier ⇔	Suspect reaches for an unknown
Objective: Soldier may fire	*Subjective:* ?

The success or failure of operational counterterrorism is largely dependent on the specifics of this fact pattern. If the individual was indeed reaching for a weapon, then the rules of engagement would justify opening fire. Engaging the individual under such circumstances meets self-defense standards as understood in criminal and international law alike. The critical word is "if."

The example above demonstrates significant possibility for misinterpretation. In the majority of cases, the determination regarding the threat posed by an individual is best made by the soldier on the ground. However, the tragic outcome predicated on misunderstanding demands that, if possible, additional factors (such as the helicopter pilot) be included.

How much time and weight should be given to additional factors is an open question. There are clearly time and operational limits. The threat is neither abstract nor vague; it is potentially very acute and delay may result in the death of the soldier. Conversely, misreading the situation (and the threat) may result both in the killing of an innocent person (who did not pose a threat) or misfiring and killing innocent people in the immediate vicinity (collateral damage).

The fallout from collateral damage in the context of counterterrorism is significant. It is a prime example of blow back, which directly leads to additional acts of terrorism. Therefore, it is critical that commanders ascertain to the greatest extent possible whether the individual *genuinely* presents a threat. However, that determination must occur quickly and decisively because the danger to soldiers is potentially life-threatening.

2. Soldier's Conduct and Training

The principal rule of command is "know your soldier" (in additional to the fundamental rule of warfare, "know your enemy"). In determining whether to issue an open fire order, the commander must determine whether his forces are strategically positioned in the event of escalation. An open fire order cannot be viewed as an isolated incident. The commander does not necessarily know where additional danger lurks and is therefore at a significant operational disadvantage to the target.

That operational disadvantage is minimized by a combination of viable, real-time intelligence information and the unit's skill level. In preparing his soldiers for operational counterterrorism, the commander has to teach the soldier both traditional military skills (shooting, navigation) and non-traditional skills (distinguishing between civilians and legitimate targets when both wear identical clothes). If the commander is uncertain about the unit's abilities, he or she is consequently restricted regarding "open fire" orders.

This trust in the unit's abilities and training is absolutely necessary since the commander is not always in the field with the unit. If the unit requests permission to open fire and the commander is without visual equipment enabling him or her to see what the unit sees, then the decision to grant permission *must* be influenced by the unit's training and skill set.

To also ensure that the unit acts in accordance with the four international law principles (collateral damage, alternatives, proportionality, and military necessity), the unit must be operationally trained and prepared for a wide range of eventualities. While it is impossible to be prepared for *all* possibilities, it is the commander's responsibility to minimize harm to innocent civilians should he issue an "open fire" order. How is that seemingly "simple" task achieved?

3. Degree of Danger Posed

Not dissimilar from various examples in the criminal law paradigm (in particular, community reactions to perceptions of police brutality), any effective operation must take into account what effect an "open fire" order will have. This consideration reflects a strategic, rather than tactical, approach to counterterrorism. That is, if counterterrorism is viewed solely through the scope of the gun, then larger considerations will be ignored. The fall-out from such a limited analysis is enormous.

QUESTIONS TO CONSIDER

1. Does the particular community have a reputation for reacting violently to the wounding or death of a community member?
2. Is the community a known hotbed of extremism?
3. Are there respected voices of moderation in the community?
4. Is the community's location of strategic importance — politically, religiously, ethnically, socially, economically?
5. What is the relationship between the community and neighboring communities?
6. Are additional threats in the immediate vicinity? If so, are these threats immediate?

Not only must the commander seek to know who the targeted individual is, he or she must have a clear understanding regarding the community's possible reactions. The commander ignores these issues at risk. If the only consideration is the killing of a specific target, then the commander is strictly conducting tactical counterterrorism.

Can strategic counterterrorism be conducted when the commander (or his troops) is confronted with a terrorist who presents an *immediate* threat? The answer is in the question: How immediate is *immediate* and can the threat be mitigated?

Even if justified, the possible fallout from an operational decision conceivably outweighs the benefits. Therefore, it is suggested that the commander engage in strategic thinking even when in the zone of combat and confronted with a viable—yet manageable—threat. The only exception should be when the threat is expressed in the form of an individual identified beyond a reasonable doubt as an attacker (suicide bomber, shooter, stabber) who unequivocally presents an immediate danger that can only be neutralized by forceful action.

4. Unit's Previous Conduct/Experience

Not all units are fully operational for each mission they are ordered to undertake. While a commander's natural impulse is to respond affirmatively when ordered to perform a particular mission, there is an additional consideration, particularly with respect to operational counterterrorism. Unlike the traditional military paradigm pitting soldiers against soldiers, the risk of harming innocent civilians (and therefore unintentionally contributing to the escalation of violence) dramatically reinforces the need for operational preparedness and experience.

Though a unit's inexperience in the traditional war undoubtedly led to tragedy, its impact was localized and did not impact the larger picture. From the perspective of the rule of law, international law, and morality in armed conflict, the "strategic corporal" was not a factor in wars such as World War I or II. He is, however, an important factor in counterterrorism. The "strategic corporal's" lack of experience in non-traditional conflict reverberates beyond the specific conflict. The term, which has become state of art in American military parlance, refers to the strategic fallout from an operational mistake committed by the lone soldier. For a variety of reasons — media, court of international opinion, proximity to civilian populations — mistakes made by a soldier reverberate far beyond the immediate zone of combat. Hence, the term "strategic corporal."

The requirement to distinguish between the combatants and non-combatants is an absolute. That is not too suggest mistakes are not inevitable. Precisely to minimize the "strategic corporal's" impact, the commander is obligated to a larger responsibility. While targeting a terrorism suspect is important, how and when the act is performed is just as important. A military unit unfamiliar with the surrounding area, not confident in its abilities in small-arms tactics while in the midst of innocent civilians, is a recipe for disaster. To that end, open fire orders have a natural progression in how and when a unit operationally engages.

While differences exist (depending also on the particular threat presented), the general progression is as follows:

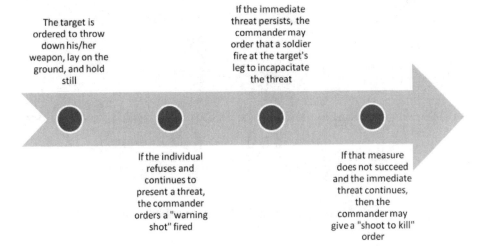

The target is ordered to throw down his/her weapon, lay on the ground, and hold still

If the immediate threat persists, the commander may order that a soldier fire at the target's leg to incapacitate the threat

If the individual refuses and continues to present a threat, the commander orders a "warning shot" fired

If that measure does not succeed and the immediate threat continues, then the commander may give a "shoot to kill" order

The above progression lasts but a few seconds. There are, however, threats so immediate (a just-detected suicide bomber) that such a progression is operationally impractical. Those situations require that the unit be operationally trained and experienced because attendant risks (short- and long-term alike) are so enormous.

During the initial phases of the Palestinian *intifada* (1987-1993), senior military officials suggested creating a full-time, permanent counterterrorism unit comprised of professional police officers rather than 19-year-old conscripts serving in the IDF. While such a unit was never established, the misconduct of soldiers placed in a situation best described as "mission impossible" justified closer examination of the proposal. Soldiers are traditionally trained to engage other soldiers; they are not trained to respond to massive demonstrations, nor stone- and Molotov cocktail–throwing on an unprecedented scale.

D. ALTERNATIVE MEANS TO NEUTRALIZE THE THREAT

Perhaps no issue better illustrates the tension between operational counterterrorism and international law obligations than "alternatives." In discussing alternatives, the suggestion is that the commander seeks to mitigate the threat posed either to his unit or innocent civilians.

Examining Alternatives

1. Who is potentially injured or killed if the alternative is not identified or applied?

2. Given the field circumstances, what are reasonable alternatives?

3. What are the rules of engagement standard operating procedures regarding alternatives?

4. What intelligence briefing did the commander receive prior to the mission?

5. What is a reasonable limit to alternative seeking? (threat immediacy from the perspective of time and severity)

A discussion regarding alternatives must include analysis of three relevant international law principles: military necessity, collateral damage, and proportionality. The obligations are symbiotically intertwined. A commander's decision to seek alternatives prior to giving an "open fire" order must take into account (consciously and deliberately) of the threat posed (military necessity), possible damage to innocent civilians (collateral damage), and weighing the potential threat (proportionality).

The alternatives dilemma must be viewed from two different perspectives: a response to an immediate, sudden threat (such as a suicide bomber) as compared to a planned operational countermission (targeted killing). In the first paradigm, the commander's time to weigh the alternatives is extremely limited and is largely based on field circumstances. In the second paradigm, the alternatives are weighed, considered, and decided upon in advance of the "open fire" order.

E. MILITARY NECESSITY AND "OPEN FIRE" ORDERS

Prior to giving an open fire order, the commander must conclude that the threat presented is so serious that no alternative exists. The critical variable in the context of military necessity is threat gravity. Similar to alternatives, the concept is not empirical and is largely dependent on the commander's interpretation and discretion. In weighing an "open fire" order in the context of "military necessity," the commander is obligated to ascertain the threat's seriousness.

How serious is *serious*? According to whose standard and criteria? This is perhaps the crux of the relationship between international law and operational counterterrorism.

EXAMPLE

> A unit has just completed a dangerous and complicated mission in the heart of enemy territory and has now gathered at the rendezvous point. One of the soldiers suddenly notices a shepherd in the distance, running away.
>
> The shepherd can potentially reveal the unit's position to the enemy before they are picked up, forcing them into an unnecessary confrontation with enemy forces. The shepherd cannot be taken with the unit. What can the commander do to stop the shepherd? Can the shepherd be killed? Do the lives of ten soldiers outweigh the life of one shepherd? Can the shepherd be shot and wounded? Tied up and left in the middle of nowhere?
>
> The answer is that all possible measures should be taken to prevent the disclosure of the unit's position without killing the shepherd, including tying him up.

F. CONCLUSION

Except in the most immediately threatening circumstances, commanders must operate in accordance with the four-step test suggested above when engaging the enemy. The "open fire" order should be viewed from multiple perspectives: the reliability of the intelligence must be weighed, the potential reaction of the community must be projected, the skill and experience of the military unit must be considered, and alternatives must be examined.

As explained in this chapter, policy and legal considerations define the parameters, and intelligence information identifies potential targets, but whether or not to open fire remains a matter of command discretion. While protecting troops and innocent civilians is critical, international and domestic law requires the commander to exercise *maximum* discretion.

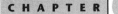
SEPARATION OF POWERS AND CHECKS AND BALANCES

A. INTRODUCTION

Separation of powers and checks and balances are both supremely important in the fight against terrorism. An unfettered executive will engage in excess, violate individual civil liberties, and possibly cause harm to foreign relations. While the executive is perhaps best-equipped to respond to an immediate threat, that does not necessarily apply to long-term policy decisions and their implications. When the executive is not reigned in by the legislative or judiciary branches, it is bound to make mistakes. If the legislature and judiciary do not engage in oversight and meaningful collaboration, the nation will have a less effective counterterrorism strategy — if only because alternatives were never articulated.

In the immediate aftermath of 9/11, Congress overwhelmingly ratified the "Authorization to Use Military Force" (AUMF). Congress failed, however, to articulate limits of the force that could be used. Congress acted, but its actions were more akin to blind support of what the executive wanted than constitutionally mandated oversight. Rather than engage the Bush Administration in debate regarding the limits of power, Congress stood by while the unfettered executive defined the debate. The U.S. Supreme Court's message to the executive was equally clear. Then-Chief Justice William Rehnquist had previously written that in times of armed conflict, the Court must be "reticent."

While Americans were urging the Administration to act, Congress and the judiciary took a backseat to the discussion regarding counterterrorism at home and abroad. If the Court is reticent to engage and Congress refrains from engaging in oversight, how are separation of powers to be implemented? Are checks and balances possible under such conditions?

Limiting executive power requires the judiciary and legislature to act proactively. Otherwise, egregious errors will go largely uncorrected and are all but sure to repeat themselves in the event of future attacks.

The theory propounded by some policy makers and academics advocating expansive executive powers in wartime has directly resulted in many of the mistakes made following 9/11. The two most prominent examples are (1) the Administration linking 9/11 to Iraq, which lead to the 2003 invasion, and (2) the torture-based interrogation regime.

"America under attack" may be an effective bumper sticker or campaign slogan; as a matter of state policy, it is fraught with danger. While an executive whose hands are so tied that the public is not protected is dangerous, it is equally vital to democratic values and principles that executive actions be subject to scrutiny and oversight.

Balance is the fundamental principle in defining what civil society is. While the public clamors for action following a terrorist attack, the executive branch's response must be both legal and moral. Otherwise, the slippery slope awaits society and government alike.

B. HOW—AND WHERE—DO WE STRIKE A BALANCE?

FIGURE 6.1   Striking a Balance

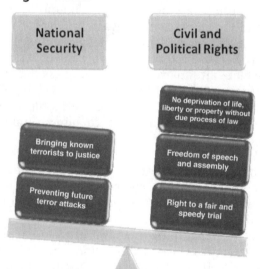

At the same time, it is important to remember that operational counterterrorism is conducted not in the marble halls of Washington, D.C. but the back alleys of Mosul and Ramallah. Therefore, the critical — perhaps only — question decision and policy makers must ask themselves is how soldiers operationally "translate" counterterrorism policy. All three branches of government must be willing to ask that question. Members of Congress must understand that protecting American servicemen requires questioning the executive branch's actions and motivations. The same holds true for the Supreme Court.

C. AHARON BARAK'S THEORY OF JUDICIAL REVIEW

According to Justice Aharon Barak, former President of the Israel Supreme Court, both the executive and the legislative branches of a democracy are directly responsive to the desires and needs of the public. However, judges are the ultimate protectors of democracy. Actions taken by the executive and the legislature must be able to withstand judicial scrutiny. Justices are not accountable to the public; they enjoy an independence that the executive and legislature do not. This independence and lack of public accountability allows justices to do what is necessary to uphold democracy, even when citizens and the State are willing to sacrifice individual rights. The role of the court is to "ensure the constitutionality and legality of the fight," regardless of whether the decisions of the court are popular with the executive or the public.[1]

According to Justice Barak, the role of a justice in protecting democracy and individual human rights is "a much more formidable duty in times of war and terrorism than in times of peace and security." It is during times of war and terrorism that citizens often think it permissible to compromise rights and protections in order to help maintain security. Justices cannot allow themselves to compromise citizens' rights, regardless of whether it is a time of war or peace. Justices cannot have different procedures or standards for wartime without eroding peacetime protections as well. Judicial decisions during times of crisis "remain with the democracy when the threat of terrorism passes...entrenched in the case law of the court as a magnet for the development of new and problematic laws." It is much easier for the executive to change directions or policy, or for the legislature to revoke, amend, or pass new laws to amend existing legislation, than for

---

1. See generally Aharon Barak, *A Judge on Judging: The Role of a Supreme Court in a Democracy*, Harvard Law Review, 2002.

the judiciary to reverse itself. Mistakes made by the judiciary live on even after they have been overruled. The logic, reasoning, and basis for a decision are recorded in judicial history to be used in the future as precedent for other cases, whereas overturned executive or legislative actions are generally ignored.

D. THE NECESSITY OF CONGRESSIONAL OVERSIGHT

Separation of powers and checks and balances are critical to governance, particularly when the executive makes decisions endangering the public's constitutional rights and soldiers' lives. While Tennyson's famous words, "Ours is not to wonder why, ours is but to do and die," may ring true with the grunt in the battlefield, neither the Supreme Court nor Congress can hide behind the façade that the executive knows all. Government owes soldiers the responsibility to ensure that they are not unnecessarily and recklessly placed in harm's way.

Checks and balances regarding operational counterterrorism are particularly critical because of the conflicts' inherent amorphousness and murkiness. The Bush Administration's consistent inability — if not unwillingness — to precisely define relevant terms highlights the need for congressional oversight. For example, in the immediate aftermath of 9/11, President Bush declared "war on terrorism." The current Chairman of the Joint Chiefs of Staff, Michael Mullen, has indicated that the phrase should no longer be used. Nonetheless, it remains a largely *unchallenged* term of art by Congress, in spite of Mullen's proclamation and its semantic and legal incorrectness.

Effective congressional oversight should lead to critical questioning regarding resource allocation, goals, missions, strategy, end game, rules of engagement, status of detainees, and methods of interrogation. What does such a conflict mandate regarding the trials of suspected terrorists? Before the executive branch commits American forces, these definitions need to be articulated with specificity.

To claim an expansive reading of presidential power is a valid constitutional argument that merits serious debate and dialogue. The leading advocates of such a philosophy include Vice President Dick Cheney, Vice President Cheney's Chief of Staff, David Addington, and Professor John Yoo. All make a compelling and cogent argument advocating their position. But neither Congress nor the Court need accept that argument at face value — indeed, they are obligated to challenge the concept and probe it for potential weaknesses.

When the President declared war on terrorism, responsible lawmakers were constitutionally obligated to demand articulation of the term. On the premise that it was a well-developed policy position, the Administration should have been required by Congress to explain its meaning. For example, does the war on terror suggest (explicitly or implicitly) that water boarding is legal? Does the phrase suggest that the Geneva Conventions are no longer applicable? Does the term mean that the U.S. may practice "rendition," whereby an uncooperative detainee is transported to a nation where torture is not illegal? This practice is forbidden by the 1984 Convention Against Torture, to which the U.S. is a signatory. Yet reliable reports indicate the U.S. has been engaging in renditions.

While the "unitary executive" doctrine propounds an expansive view of presidential powers, "on the ground" reality must be subject to congressional oversight and judicial review. The possibilities for mistakes — not to mention the cost emanating from potential mistakes — are too significant.

In November 2001, President Bush issued a Presidential Order creating military tribunals to be held in Guantanamo Bay for detainees captured overseas following 9/11. In December 2001 and January 2002, the Senate Judiciary and Armed Services Committees held hearings regarding the tribunals. When then–Attorney General John Ashcroft testified before the Judiciary Committee, Committee chairman Sen. Patrick Leahy (D-VT) told the Attorney General that he was aware of the tribunals solely because his wife had a subscription to the *Washington Post*. While perhaps meant partially in jest, the comment highlights the practical effect of the unitary executive.

Had Congress and the Administration collaborated, the judicial process (detention to trial) would not be the failure it is today. Figure 6.2 lists some of the more prominent policy failures of Guantanamo Bay.

FIGURE 6.2 Guantanamo Bay Detainees

Questionable Arrests	Indefinite Detentions	No Meaningful Convictions
Of the initial 720 detainees held in Guantanamo Bay, hundreds have been released over the past six years. Primarily, they have been released because their initial detention was unwarranted both because of insufficient intelligence and ambiguous criteria justifying the detention. Congressional oversight could have addressed these issues by *at least* posing relevant questions to Administration officials.	Detention is but a first step — it is necessary to determine whether cause exists for *continuing* detention. By not consulting with Congress, the Administration established an "indefinite detention" regime. While some argue that 9/11 justified detaining (indefinitely) the "worst of the worst," that begs the larger issue. Thomas Paine's words, "He that would make his own liberty secure must guard even his enemy from oppression; for if he violates this duty he establishes a precedent that will reach to himself" are particularly applicable to this paradigm.	As these lines are written, only two Guantanamo Bay detainees have been convicted. David Hicks' conviction was the result of a plea bargain which included release to his homeland of Australia without incarceration; Salim Hamdan was acquitted and convicted with respect to changes filed against him.

Would congressional oversight have guaranteed that a fundamentally flawed policy not be articulated or implemented? Obviously, there are no guarantees, but when the Founding Fathers established checks and balances, their primary purpose was to ensure oversight of such decisions. The most vociferous opposition to the Administration's proposal interrogation methods policies came from the Judge Advocate Generals of the military's four branches—Army, Navy, Air Force, and Marines. While the White House was urging, advocating, and implementing a torture-based interrogation regime, the military was urging restraint, caution, and limited interrogation.

The Judge Advocate Generals (hereinafter TJAGs) are first and foremost commanders. They and their fellow commanders understand the ramifications of the Administration's policy should American servicemen and women fall into captivity. According to the four TJAGs and other senior commanders, the Administration's policy all but guarantees that American personnel would be tortured to death if captured in Iraq. While some have argued that torture of American soldiers would inevitably occur, senior commanders are convinced that the Administration's policy guarantees it.

Perhaps commanders understood that painful reality in a way senior Administration officials could not. In addition to their role as commanders, the four TJAGs are also responsible for ensuring that the military is subservient to the rule of law. While the Administration was engaged in unilaterally articulating new rules of international law—including an argument that the Geneva Convention was inapplicable to the post-9/11 world—senior military attorneys were making efforts to ensure the rule of law was upheld.

The criticism offered only by the TJAGs and other high level commanders should have been offered by Congress as well. Because Congress was not engaged in active checks and balances—some would argue it barely met a standard of passivity—the burden fell on the military. In other words, external (Congress) checks were not imposed on the Administration that was subjected only to internal (military) checks. Arguably, this lack of checks and balances significantly contributed to failed and illegal conterterrorism measures. In the following table, the three policy measures of the Bush Administration illustrate how an unfettered executive branch can result in dangerous excesses.

Authorization for Use of Military Force in Response to the 9/11 Attacks[2]	A joint resolution by Congress authorized the President to "use all necessary and appropriate force against those nations, organizations or persons he determines planned, authorized, committed or aided the terrorist attacks that occurred on September 11, 2002, or harbored such organizations or persons." It was signed into law on September 18, 2001.
USA PATRIOT Act[3]	Signed into law on October 26, 2001, the Uniting and Strengthening America by Providing Appropriate Tools Required to Intercept and Obstruct Terrorism Act of 2001 substantially expanded the authority of U.S. law enforcement agencies for the stated purpose of fighting terrorism in the United States and abroad. Ironically, the 9/11 Commission Report would later indicate that law enforcement officials had all the power they had needed to stop the attacks on the Pentagon, World Trade Center, and Pennsylvania, but for various reasons had not foreseen the attacks.
Military Commissions Act of 2006[4]	After the Supreme Court's decision in *Hamdan v. Rumsfeld*, Congress passed the MCA, which was signed into law on October 17, 2006. The Act's stated purpose is to "facilitate bringing to justice terrorists and other unlawful enemy combatants through full and fair trials by military commissions, and for other purposes."

What do the congressional Acts in response to 9/11 suggest? The Authorization for Use of Military Force leaves all defining power in the executive's domain — "use all necessary force against those...he determines planned, authorized," etc. This statute has led to an extraordinary expansion of presidential power; as an example, it has been cited as authority to engage in electronic surveillance against possible terrorists without prior authorization from the FISA Court, though legislation requires such preliminary authorization (with retroactive warrants permissible in certain circumstances).

The suggestion is clear: Congress has not been actively engaged in its constitutionally mandated role of checks and balances, and has instead adopted an approach best described as complicit, if not acquiescent. When this happens, the burden falls on the judiciary. If both are overly deferential, the burden falls on either the public or the media.

---

2. Pub. L. No. 107-40, 115 Stat. 224 (2001).
3. Pub. L. No. 107-56, 115 Stat. 272 (2001).
4. Pub. L. No. 109-366, 120 Stat. 260 (2006).

1. The Judiciary

The U.S. Supreme Court has not been as acquiescent as the U.S. Congress. The Court recently decided *Boumediene v. Bush*, a challenge both of the detention of Lakhadar Boumediene and the Military Commissions Act of 2006. The Court held that enemy combatants held at Guantanamo had the right to habeas corpus, and therefore that the MCA provision denying habeas was unconstitutional.[5]

While *Boumediene* can be considered a step in the right direction regarding active judicial review of the executive, it is important to note that the case was decided years after the first detainees were imprisoned at Guantanamo Bay. The Court's reluctance to hear Guantanamo cases, as well as the 5-4 ruling with dissenting justices offering blistering criticisms of the majority opinion reflects the hands-off approach regarding judicial review during armed conflict advocated by late Chief Justice Rehnquist.[6] In large part the Bush Administration's post-9/11 policies were unchecked by the Court which acted hesitatingly and not in a timely fashion.

2. The Public

The American public's reaction to 9/11 can best be described as deferring to the President's call to a war on terrorism. While perhaps understandable from an emotional perspective, this did not contribute to lawful nor effective counterterrorism. The instinctual desire for revenge consistently articulated to the Administration suggested that "by all means necessary" is both demanded and accepted. While perhaps understandable given the enormity of 9/11, American history is replete with examples of excess in response to an attack on America. The internment of Japanese-Americans in Pearl Harbor's aftermath is but the most egregious of overreactions on all levels: the public, the FDR Administration, and the Supreme Court.[7]

---

5. Boumediene v. Bush, 553 U.S. _____ (2008).

6. WILLIAM H. REHNQUIST, ALL THE LAWS BUT ONE, PATRICIA HASS ED. (Alfred Knopf, 1998).

7. Korematsu v. United States, 323 U.S. 214 (1944), is an infamous Supreme Court case where, in a 6-3 decision, the Court upheld the constitutionality of Executive Order 9066, which required the interment of Japanese-Americans in the Western United States. The majority reasoned that the need to protect the nation's security outweighed the individual rights of Americans of Japanese descent. Justice Frank Murphy dissented, saying that the treatment of Japanese-Americans amounted to racism and compared the U.S.'s actions to that of Nazi Germany. Justice Robert Jackson also dissented, albeit in less strong terms, writing that even if the courts should not be put in the position of second-guessing the decisions of military commanders, that does not mean that judges should ratify orders that are unconstitutional. *Korematsu* has never been explicitly overturned.

3. The Media

With respect to the American media, the terms that best describe post-9/11 coverage are complicity, acquiescence, and deference. Whether the lack of critical commentary was a reflection of jingoism or a response to public fervor is beyond the purview of this book. What is clear, however, is that the Administration was largely given a free pass by the American media following the attacks on the World Trade Center and the Pentagon.

4. Executive Self-Restraint

If the Supreme Court (reticence in the face of armed attack), Congress (deferential/complicit), the public (desire for revenge), and the media (deferential/complicit) are not going to engage in active checks and balances, how is the Administration to be restrained? The only force in society left to check the executive is the executive itself.

Should terrorism not be met by an *unrestrained* attack? In analyzing the issue of restraint — the core of checks and balances — three approaches are suggested. See Figure 6.3.

FIGURE 6.3 Restraints

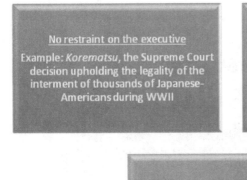

When other branches fail to fulfill their roles, the executive branch must impose restraints on itself. An executive that fails to do so will violate core civil democratic values and principles. That does, however, beg question as to whether terrorism justifies reducing constitutional privileges and protections. If so, whose privileges and rights are reduced?

One of the most difficult and important questions is whether those accused of attacking the U.S. should be granted constitutional rights. As human beings, they are obviously granted *some* rights, but how far do those rights extend? The principles and questions in Figure 6.4 are inherent to the discussion.

Is an objective approach to counterterrorism possible, or are counterterrorism and terrorist threats best understood subjectively? In the absence of rigorous (much less passive) checks and balances, the executive must address these questions alone. The self-imposed theory requires that it be done from the perspectives illustrated in Figure 6.5.

The self-imposed theory presumes that terrorism cannot be defeated and therefore the executive must assume a long-term perspective regarding the threat. If terrorism cannot be defeated — only managed or minimized — what are the limits on operational counterterrorism? According to the self-imposed limits theory, the answer is in the question.

FIGURE 6.4 Rights of the Accused

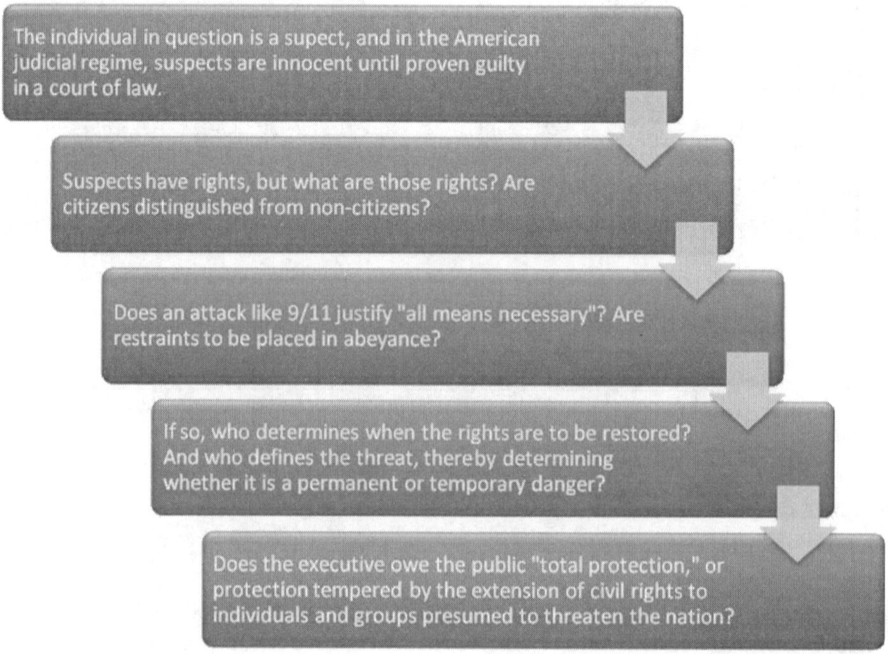

The individual in question is a supect, and in the American judicial regime, suspects are innocent until proven guilty in a court of law.

Suspects have rights, but what are those rights? Are citizens distinguished from non-citizens?

Does an attack like 9/11 justify "all means necessary"? Are restraints to be placed in abeyance?

If so, who determines when the rights are to be restored? And who defines the threat, thereby determining whether it is a permanent or temporary danger?

Does the executive owe the public "total protection," or protection tempered by the extension of civil rights to individuals and groups presumed to threaten the nation?

FIGURE 6.5   Self-Imposed Theory

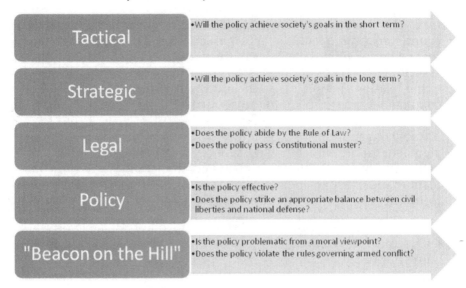

Tactical	•Will the policy achieve society's goals in the short term?
Strategic	•Will the policy achieve society's goals in the long term?
Legal	•Does the policy abide by the Rule of Law? •Does the policy pass Constitutional muster?
Policy	•Is the policy effective? •Does the policy strike an appropriate balance between civil liberties and national defense?
"Beacon on the Hill"	•Is the policy problematic from a moral viewpoint? •Does the policy violate the rules governing armed conflict?

The following examples—drawing on specific events—highlight the decision-making processes regarding checks and balances and restraint (external or internal) on the executive.

Example 1

In the aftermath of an attack in which a number of Israelis were shot by terrorists who used trees for cover, a senior military commander ordered their razing. During in-the-field discussion, the commander made a sweeping gesture with his hand and said, "Take those trees down." When asked what does "those" mean, he gestured "over there."

The response was deemed insufficient on multiple levels: those who actually had to raze the trees were unclear regarding the operational significance of "over there," and I (the legal advisor) was concerned that the decision could not be "explained" to the Israeli Supreme Court sitting as the High Court of Justice as it was lacking in specificity. In American legal terms, it would be defined as "void for vagueness." When the commander understood that the razing would require specifically marking the area to be affected, he withdrew his order.

The decision is a direct reflection of internal restraints; the commander understood that the cost of staff work required for implementation far outweighed any benefit accrued in a cost-benefit analysis. In addition, the commander was not convinced that the Court would uphold his decision if attorney's filed a petition challenging its legality.

Example 2

In 1997, a senior commander determined to engage in a particular counterterrorism operation. When asked for my advice, I responded that while the proposal was legal, the operation should be cancelled, as its long-term policy implications would negatively affect the developing relations between the IDF and the Palestinian Authority. The commander ordered planning to go forth.

At my request, the commander agreed to meet with me for a private conversation; I was granted "permission to speak freely." My argument for recommending mission cancellation was a combination of law and policy, with an emphasis on the latter. While the commander indicated at the end of our conversation that he was going forth, the mission was cancelled shortly thereafter.

Did my conversation "sway" the commander? A couple of years later I asked the commander; in spite of our personal friendship, he chose not to answer.

Example 3

A senior commander decided to implement a policy that would impose unwarranted and unjustifiable restrictions of movement on a particular population category. I explained to the commander that his decision would not pass judicial muster and that the High Court of Justice would rule the action violates basic civil rights of the affected population group.

The commander argued that security considerations justified his decision, convinced that his actions would save lives. It was suggested to the commander that less severe actions be considered, but the commander insisted that there were no alternatives.

Ultimately, the commander reversed himself and decided not to implement the security measure. What convinced the commander was the argument that not only would the High Court rule against him, but would do so in such a manner as to publicly rebuke, if not embarrass, him — and by extension, the IDF.

Example 4

In response to Palestinian terrorism, the IDF sealed or demolished the homes (rented or owned) of those suspected of terrorist activity in accordance with Article 119 of the Defense Emergency Regulations, 1945. Historically, the High Court of Justice upheld commander's decisions regarding the measure.

In the 1990s, however, the Court adopted a more critical approach and increasingly narrowed the circumstances in which the measure could be implemented. While the executive (IDF commanders) argued the measure deterred Palestinians from engaging in terrorism, the High Court concluded the sanction was "broad in scope." In response, the IDF initially limited demolition only to those homes owned by the terrorists before concluding that the measure did not have the desired deterrence effect.

What is important to note in the last example is that the Court's intervention was in "real time"; the hearings before the Court were scheduled shortly after the executive decided on a particular course of action. Unlike the U.S. Supreme Court, which has responded hesitatingly to the military tribunals established in Guantanamo Bay, the Israeli Supreme Court has implemented an active judicial review of executive action.

E. CONCLUSION

Operational counterterrorism is the world of dark shadows and back alleys. It is an extraordinarily complicated effort to neutralize a largely unseen enemy. The executive branch is simultaneously on the offensive and defensive with respect to future attacks. The price of a successful terrorist attack is known to all: innocent civilians injured and killed, a public demanding an immediate response, and a media that is largely quick to judge the government's failure to prevent the attack.

In a democracy, failure to adequately protect the public can quickly lead to defeat at the polls. However, or perhaps because of that, the government's response may well be excessive and violate the rights of the individual. While national security is important, it is not, as Barak argues, an absolute. In his words, national security is not a magical phrase that justifies government misconduct in the context of civil and political rights.

However, as repeatedly evidenced, government excess is an oft-repeated occurrence in response to an act of terrorism. How to minimize excess is critical to a civil, democratic society that believes in the rule of law. Minimizing excess, however, is not a given. The executive may not limit itself. Separation of powers and checks and balances requires that "limiting excess" be the result of active oversight and review by the legislature and courts. Otherwise, the rights of individuals may be violated in the name of national security.

In seeking to ensure that the executive does not violate the rights of innocent suspects, additional, non-traditional checks and balances need be developed and implemented. This is particularly the case if the legislature and courts do not meet their obligation. While clearing the playing field for the executive may *seem* effective in response to an act of terrorism, a long-term strategic analytical perspective clearly suggests otherwise.

CHAPTER 7

INTERROGATION OF TERRORISM SUSPECTS

A. INTRODUCTION

Intelligence gathering is perhaps the most important aspect of counter-terrorism. Intelligence can come from a wide range of sources — open sources such as the media and the Internet, electronic sources including wiretaps, and human sources. Getting information from a human source can be relatively easy when the source is willing, or it can be difficult, particularly when the source is a suspected terrorist. The ultimate question is whether terrorism — or the threat of terrorism — justifies torturing an individual suspected of involvement in an attack.

The recent Army Field Manual, as well as the Military Commissions Act, explicitly forbids U.S. soldiers from torturing detainees. Neither prohibition applies to CIA personnel, nor to foreign interrogators acting at the behest of the CIA. Furthermore, President Bush's stock response to whether U.S. personnel torture is an unequivocal denial — followed by a promise that all measures necessary will be taken to protect Americans.

What is the consequence of making such qualified statements? In his confirmation hearings before the Senate Judiciary Committee, Attorney General–nominee Michael Mukasey refused to answer specific questions regarding torture. While agreeing with members of the panel that torture is unconstitutional, Mukasey hedged on actual interrogation measures themselves. This approach is a sure-fire means for ensuring the continued mistreatment of detainees by American personnel.

In order for operational counterterrorism to be effective and legal, instructions must be crystal-clear. Mixed messages are problematic in any aspect of human endeavor, particularly when acting on them may result in loss of life or injury, not to mention violations of domestic and international law.

To satisfactorily engage in this discussion requires carefully defining the limits of interrogation. Otherwise, those who wish to skirt around the law will take advantage of the subsequent nebulousness. In addition, the issue of torture is directly related to the essence of a polity, for it defines society's fundamental core values.

B. WHEN MESSAGES ARE MIXED: ABU GHRAIB

At Abu Ghraib prison in Iraq, detainees were mistreated by interrogators and detention center personnel. Reports indicate that detainees were urinated on, burned with phosphoric acid, and sodomized with batons. One prisoner's leg was repeatedly jumped on; as a result, it improperly healed from gunshot wounds. Prisoners were dragged across the floor by ropes tied to their legs and genitalia. Additional photos and video revealed evidence of prisoners threatened with snarling dogs and forced to have sex with each other. Prisoners reported that the guards threatened them and their families with murder and rape. It is irrelevant from a moral standpoint whether or not the mistreated prisoners were guilty. However, Colonel Janis Karpinski, the commander of Abu Ghraib, later estimated that 90 percent of detainees were innocent.[1]

In the 1984 Convention Against Torture (CAT), torture is defined as the infliction of severe mental or physical pain. The War Crimes Act of 1996 made torture and other inhumane treatment of prisoners a felony. One would think that both international and domestic U.S. law were clear on these points—so how could Abu Ghraib have occurred?

Army Reserve Staff Sgt. Chip Frederick—a participant in the abuse—would later tell CBS News, "We had no support, no training whatsoever, and I kept asking my chain of command for certain things...like rules and regulations...and it just wasn't happening."[2]

Abu Ghraib presents a critical lesson for counterterrorism students. When the rules of interrogation are not articulated, abuse will occur. Abuses resulted from the lack of clarity offered by those who seek to parse and qualify the definition of torture. What reasons would policy makers have for keeping the definition of torture vague? What benefit is there to narrow the definition? Regardless of the definition, "torture" is forbidden and the fact that the definition remains unclear means the

---

1. Jen Banbury, "Rummy's Scapegoat," SALON, Nov. 10, 2005.

2. "Iraqi abuse photos spark outrage," BBC News, April 30, 2004, *available at* http://news.bbc.co.uk/2/hi/middle_east/3672901.stm. *See also* "'I asked for help and warned of this but nobody would listen,'" THE GUARDIAN, May 1, 2004, *available at* http://www.guardian.co.uk/world/2004/may/01/iraq1/.

limits of interrogation are unclear to those who need them most: the interrogators. Simply stated, torture is illegal, immoral, and does not lead to actionable (defined as information that can be "operationalized") intelligence.

Professor Alan Dershowitz advocates "controlling and limiting the use of torture by means of a warrant or some other mechanism of accountability."[3] While this proposal conceivably sounds attractive—judicial authorization—it must be rejected, for its ultimate purpose is to authorize torture. Though the proposal is justified on the "ticking time bomb" theory,[4] the reality of the proposal cannot be denied—it grants interrogators the right to violate international and domestic law. In addition, the fundamental premise of the "ticking time bomb" must be treated with enormous skepticism, if not downright rejection.

C. WHAT TECHNIQUES ARE PERMISSIBLE?

Whether they knew it or not, interrogators at Abu Ghraib were acting in accordance with former Attorney General Gonzales' characterization of the Geneva Conventions as "quaint." Furthermore, the Bybee-Yoo memos justified torture short of organ failure. Torture has no place in a civil, democratic state—it cannot be justified legally, morally, ethically, or even from a Machiavellian "ends justify the means" effectiveness standpoint. Studies have shown that interrogations involving torture do not result in actionable intelligence.

That is not to suggest that interrogation methods do not, and should not, include discomfort to the interrogatee. Quite the opposite—causing the interrogatee disorientation, sensory deprivation, loss of control, and discomfort are legitimate tools in an effort to receive information regarding past and future attacks.

The question is one of limits. Discussing interrogation methods requires decision and policy makers, the public, academics, and the media to articulate the limits of power. The three following tables illustrate differing approaches to acceptable and unacceptable methods of interrogation.

---

3. Amos N. Guiora, Constitutional Limits on Coercive Interrogation 121 (2008).
4. The "ticking time bomb" theory suggests that only one detainee possesses the relevant information to prevent a major terrorist attack and that all means are justified in getting that information from him.

The American Psychological Association[5]

UNACCEPTABLE METHODS	ACCEPTABLE METHODS
In 2007 the APA voted to cease participation and report involvement in the following interrogation techniques: mock executions, stress positions, sleep deprivation, simulated drowning, sexual and religious humiliation, forced nakedness, the exploitation of prisoners' phobias, the use of mind-altering drugs, hooding, the use of dogs to frighten detainees, exposing prisoners to extreme temperatures, physical assault, and threatening a prisoner or a prisoner's family.	The APA rejected a stronger resolution that would have prohibited all psychologist involvement in interrogations at U.S. detention centers. It echoed the Bush administration by condemning some techniques — isolation, sleep deprivation, sensory deprivation, or over-stimulation — only when they are likely to cause lasting harm.

European Court of Human Rights, *Ireland v. United Kingdom*[6]

UNACCEPTABLE METHODS
Five techniques of sensory deprivation — stress positions, hooding, sleep deprivation, food and drink deprivation, noise modulation — exercised at a high level constituted "inhuman and degrading treatment," if not torture. The Attorney-General of the United Kingdom later announced "that the 'five techniques' will not in any circumstances be reintroduced as an aid to interrogation."

---

5. Shanker Vedantam, "APA Rules on Interrogation Abuse," WASHINGTON POST, August 20, 2007 at A03.

6. Republic of Ireland v. United Kingdom, 2 Eur. Ct. H.R. 25.

Army Field Manual 34-52[7]

UNACCEPTABLE METHODS	ACCEPTABLE METHODS
Physical torture is defined as including tactics such as "any form of beating" or "forcing an individual to stand, sit or kneel in abnormal positions for prolonged periods of time." Stripping soldiers, keeping them in stressful positions for a long time, imposing dietary restrictions, employing police dogs to intimidate prisoners and using sleep deprivation.	Outlines acceptable techniques under five different categories—direct, incentive-based, emotional, increased fear, and pride and ego. For example, in the "emotional" category, there are "emotional-love" approaches, such as appealing to the source's desire to communicate with family or more quickly end a conflict "to save his comrade's lives."

How is it that a state action banned by international convention has made a comeback in recent years? Or perhaps the more appropriate question is, how does the U.S. justify an interrogation method that has been banned by law and castigated by moralists alike? Is this a double standard, particularly in light of consistent State Department criticism of regimes that torture?

In suggesting that torture is necessary—while denying it is occurring—the Bush Administration suggests such methods are necessary to protect American citizens. From what threat? "Threats" is a problematic term—threats are loosely defined, based on intelligence information unavailable to public and media scrutiny. They are largely, if not exclusively, within the executive domain. Assertions made by the executive branch with respect to particular threats (or what are claimed to be threats) are out of the public view. Oversight is extremely difficult, and in seeking to prevent threats from reaching fruition, excess may well occur. That excess particularly plays out in the interrogation setting. How, then, does civil democratic society balance between the need for information and the requirement to protect the rights of the detainee?

A preliminary question is whether terrorism justifies the narrowing of individual rights. While civil rights organizations instinctively advocate limiting government power even in the face of "threats," perhaps the executive's responsibility to protect the public is ultimately more important than any legal or moral considerations.

---

7. Available at http://www.globalsecurity.org/intell/library/policy/army/fm/fm34-52/toc.htm.

D. THE LEGAL IMPLICATIONS OF TORTURE: THE ADMISSIBILITY OF CONFESSIONS AT TRIAL

EXAMPLE

> I was assigned to prosecute a defendant charged with a terrorism-related crime. The defendant argued that his confession to an interrogator from the Israeli General Security Service was involuntary. Specifically, the defendant claimed the interrogator had applied unlawful, coercive measures.
>
> In accordance with the Israeli legal system, a defendant who claims that a confession was obtained through illegal means requests a "trial within a trial" exclusively for the purpose of determining its admissibility. In preparing for the hearing, I read the statement and the interrogator's report of the interrogation. As the lead prosecutor, I had to determine whether there was validity to the defendant's claim. As neither the judge nor I had been present when the interrogator interrogated the defendant, my decision would be based on a complex set of circumstantial evidence.
>
> This scenario is a classic "he said, she said" situation in that the only relevant witnesses are the two individuals claiming fundamentally contrasting versions of the same event. The interrogator did not dispute nor contradict the defendant's statement that the two had been alone during the course of the interrogation.
>
> When asked by the Judge how I intended to proceed, I decided to withdraw the charge sheet regarding those crimes to which the defendant claimed he had involuntarily confessed. In essence, the defendant's claims carried the day.

My decision in the example above was based on a number of considerations:

1. Did I think the court would find the interrogator believable?
2. Did the defendant's claims sound valid and viable?
3. How had the Court previously ruled regarding similar claims?
4. What was my "gut instinct" regarding the interrogator?
5. Were the defendant's crimes sufficiently serious to warrant addressing the claims of involuntary confession?
6. What were the consequences of dropping certain charges?

What is important to emphasize is that there are no right answers and the questions cannot be addressed in a black-white, absolute fashion. That is the essence of interrogation.

In my capacity as a judge in the Gaza Strip Military Court, I was asked to rule on admissibility issues. When a leading Gaza Strip attorney requested a hearing contesting the admissibility of his client's purported confession, I decided to visit the detention center. It was important to see firsthand the various measures the defendant claimed he had been subjected to:

- A small room termed "refrigerator" as the temperature could be modulated by the guards;
- Small chairs in which the defendant was forced to sit in a "stress position";
- Hoods placed over the defendants' heads intended to disorient and prevent contact between suspects awaiting interrogation;
- Loud and cacophonous music intended to disorient and prevent communication between suspects awaiting interrogation;
- Rings on the ceiling for purposes of causing great physical pain by forcing the defendant to "extend" his arms.

In order to ensure that the defendants' rights were preserved, I invited the prosecutor and defense counsel to both join me. The defense attorney eagerly accepted my invitation. The prosecutor declined. I assume he had previously seen the detention center. Nevertheless, his decision was regrettable, as it would have enabled him to see the center through the defense counsel's eyes.

In my ruling outlining the purpose and parameter of the visit, I held that a senior interrogator would accompany us and answer all questions asked either by counsel or myself. The interrogator was under oath during the visit and therefore answers such as "I cannot answer because of state security considerations" would be subject both to objection by counsel and Court ruling.

A detention center is inherently unpleasant: crowded, hot, sweaty, loud, and anxiety-ridden. It is not, however, necessarily nor explicitly a "torture center." The interrogator has a clear mission — getting information out of the detainee. How he or she gets that information and what means he or she uses are critical to the discussion.

While emphasizing the interrogator's means and methods, the psychology of the interrogatee is equally important. By claiming "illegal means," the detainee is conceivably saving face in his or her own community. He can tell people if not for the "torture," he would never have confessed. As a judge, I was skeptical of the assertion that torture was systematic, as claimed by some detainees and emphatically asserted by various human rights organizations. At the same time, I believed that problematic, if not clearly illegal, methods were used on occasion. The question from a philosophical and intellectual perspective was how to balance between the rights of the individual and the rights of the state.

The question from a practical perspective was whether to allow admission of the confession.

The two—intellectual and practical—are not unrelated; grappling with the balancing dilemma can facilitate a judicial ruling. The balancing dilemma is fraught with danger, for excess endangers a free society. The phrase "by all means necessary" is a sure-fire guarantee for violating the rights of the individual—some innocent, others not. Nevertheless, until proven otherwise by a court of law, civil democratic society views all people as innocent. But what happens when the interrogator is convinced that the detainee is holding something back that would either prevent a future attack or led to the arrest of those responsible for a previous one?

Some interrogation methods are blatantly illegal, but how does the trier of fact know which methods were used? How does the judge know—frankly—who is lying? In the case before me, while I had conducted an "on-site" visit with defense counsel and a senior interrogator, I had not been present during the actual interrogation. Following the on-site visit, the interrogators who had conducted the actual interrogation and were now accused of misconduct, testified before me in the "mini-trial." Their testimony was predictable—they denied all the defendant's claims.

What, then, swayed me to rule the confession inadmissible? In response to my question regarding interrogations in general—"Have you previously, or ever, engaged in methods the defense is claiming in this case?"—the interrogator categorically denied. Yet some of the methods claimed by the defendant were so innocuous that I knew they had surely been used at some point, and to deny it was absurd. That all-encompassing denial led me to rule that the defendant's confession to that particular interrogator was inadmissible.

While not ruling that all of the defendant's confessions (he gave a number) were inadmissible, I ruled in the defendant's favor with respect to one specific interrogator whose testimony I found unreliable. Was my ruling wrong? It is difficult to assess (both then and today 20 years later) because the lack of clearly articulated limits and the all-pervasive shroud of secrecy significantly inhibit careful analysis of interrogation methods.

E. THE LIMITS OF U.S. INTERROGATION POLICY

1. In the Absence of Clarity

The law is clear: torture is illegal. But what is the significance of Attorney-General nominee Mukasey's testimony that he is unfamiliar with water-boarding? While greeted with general disbelief by members of the U.S. Senate Judiciary Committee, the significance of the testimony is clear.

By pleading ignorance, Mukasey is enabling — directly or indirectly — continued torture of detainees' held by the U.S.

This is neither a vague argument nor concern; the inability or unwillingness to directly address specific interrogation methods contributes to the continued violation of human and civil rights. This is particularly problematic and troubling as the U.S. holds either directly or indirectly — as these lines are written — approximately 25,000 terrorist-related detainees worldwide. The issue of detainee rights and the limits of interrogation extend far beyond Guantanamo Bay and the now-infamous pictures from Abu Ghraib.

Seven years after 9/11, neither the Supreme Court nor Congress has actively or effectively forced the Administration to articulate the limits of interrogation. The Supreme Court in *Hamdan v. Rumsfeld* ruled that particular aspects of the Military Commissions were unconstitutional. However, the Military Commissions Act was legislated in response to *Hamdan* and created a loophole whereby CIA personnel — unlike U.S. military personnel — could torture detainees.

2. The Limits of Detention

What is the impact of a policy best described as a "wink and a nod"? While facilitating continued mistreatment of unprotected detainees, it does not guarantee effective counterterrorism. In discussing detainee interrogation, it is important to recall who the detainees are. Amnesty International estimates that of the 775 detainees brought to Guantanamo Bay, 345 were released without *any* charges brought against them by the United States as of December 2007.[8] In addition, until the Supreme Court imposed combatant status review tribunals on the Administration to determine whether a particular detainee presented a continuing threat to America's national security, no such mechanism existed.

The failure was twofold: in numerous cases, the actual threat posed by a particular individual was unclear and whether a *continuing* threat existed was beyond independent review.

In response to uncorroborated intelligence information from sources that in retrospect were of dubious reliability, the U.S. military detained individuals for alleged involvement in terrorism activity. With extraordinarily unclear guidelines as to *who* could be initially detained and subjected to *additional* detention, interrogators were interrogating individuals conceivably uninvolved in terrorist-related activities. The lack of standards combined with an absence of review standards ensured that the detention

---

8. *USA: Close Guantanamo — A Symbol of Injustice*, Amnesty International, January 1, 2007, *available at* https://www.amnesty.org/en/library/asset/AMR51/001/2007/en/dom-AMR510012007en.html/.

centers were filled with individuals who should not have been *initially* detained.

From the interrogator's perspective, this reality was problematic, if not tragic. Ordered to interrogate individuals from a culture about which he or she knew little, the interrogator was given extraordinarily broad parameters to get information someone in the chain of command believed the detainee possessed.

Without intelligence information, the state is incapable of developing and implementing operational counterterrorism measures. Gathering intelligence information requires developing a reliable source network that augments sophisticated signal intelligence. One does not come at the expense of the other, and it is all but impossible to conduct effective counterterrorism without both. While the U.S. may possess state-of-the-art electronic surveillance equipment, the lack of a broad network of sources providing reliable, valid, and viable intelligence information ultimately suggests that the intelligence gathering process is limited.

This limited intelligence gathering ability results in detainees who may, in all likelihood, not present a threat to a nation's security. As a result, their interrogation is inherently fruitless. If not involved in terrorism, how can a detainee provide relevant information to the interrogator?

Herein lays a great tension: If the detainee is uninvolved, *but* the interrogator is convinced that he or she is, then the application of unlawful interrogating measures is a very real possibility. On what basis would the interrogator reach the conclusion that the detainee poses relevant information? Largely on what a source has reported with respect to that particular individual. However, as evidenced by the large number of detainees released from Guantanamo Bay, information provided by many sources was inaccurate, misleading, or just plain wrong.

F. WHAT IS TORTURE?

Is it an exaggeration to argue that the actions of Lynndie England and her cohorts in Abu Ghraib are akin to the waterboarding to which some detainees were subjected? Waterboarding (which Vice President Cheney has infamously and gratuitously referred to as a "dunk in the water") subjects the detainee to a sensation of impending death. Forced masturbation (which was also videotaped), while unimaginably humiliating, does not suggest immediate death. Why, then, is it considered a form of torture? Are we potentially "exaggerating" how torture is defined? After all, intelligence information must be received in order to prevent future attacks and individuals responsible for previous attacks must be punished.

THE INTERNATIONAL COVENANT ON CIVIL AND POLITICAL RIGHTS

Torture is "any act by which severe pain or suffering, whether physical or mental, is intentionally inflicted on a person for such purposes as obtaining from him or a third person information or a confession, punishing him for an act he or a third person committed or is suspected of having committed, or intimidating or coercing him or a third person, or for any reason based on discrimination of any kind, when such pain or suffering is inflicted by or at the instigation of or with the consent or acquiescence of a public official or other person acting in an official capacity. It does not include pain or suffering arising only from, inherent in or incidental to lawful sanctions."

18 U.S.C. §2340 DEFINITIONS

1. "Torture" means an act committed by a person acting under the color of law specifically intended to inflict severe physical or mental pain or suffering (other than pain or suffering incidental to lawful sanctions) upon another person within his custody or physical control;
2. "Severe mental pain of suffering" means the prolonged mental harm caused by or resulting from—
   A.   The intentional inflicting or threatened infliction of severe physical pain or suffering;
   B.   The administration or application, or threatened administration or application, of mind-altering substances or other procedures calculated to disrupt profoundly the senses or the personality;
   C.   The threat of imminent death; or
   D.   The threat that another person will be imminently be subjected to death, severe physical pain or suffering, or the administration or application of mind-altering substances or other procedures calculated to disrupt profoundly the senses or personality.

THE CONVENTION AGAINST TORTURE

For the purposes of this Convention, the term "torture" means any act by which severe pain or suffering, whether physical or mental, is intentionally inflicted on a person for such purposes as obtaining from him or a third person information or a confession, punishing him for an act he or a third person has committed or is suspected of having committed, or intimidating or coercing him or a third person, or for any reason based on discrimination of any kind, when such pain or suffering is inflicted by or at the instigation of or with the consent or acquiescence of a public official or other person acting in an official capacity. It does not include pain or suffering arising only from, inherent in or incidental to lawful sanctions.

In defining torture, what weight should be given to cultural relativism? In 2005, *Newsweek* magazine reported that guards at Guantanamo Bay flushed a Koran down the toilet. Afterward, it was unclear whether the event had actually occurred, as *Newsweek*'s source was later shown to be unreliable.[9] But what if it had? The act of flushing a Koran down the toilet undoubtedly causes a truly devoted Muslim mental suffering and anguish. However, does it reach the level of torture as is associated with endless beatings, electric shock, and eye-gouging? If the tables were reversed, would the flushing of religious scriptures in the presence of a devout Christian or Jewish detainee be defined as torture?

Cultural relativism suggests subjectivity rather than objectivity. One person's tolerance to mental or physical pain tolerance is not necessarily the same as another's. A professional athlete can withstand pain quantifiably different than the casual jogger. Shun Fujimoto performed at the 1972 Olympics with a broken knee, completing his event on the rings and scoring a 9.7 for Japan. Similarly, Kerri Strug, despite suffering from a serious ankle injury, stuck her vault landing in the 1996 Olympics, assuring the American team its first Olympic team gold medal. Does this mean that a Shun Fujimoto or a Kerri Strug could be treated worse than the average detainee without the interrogation being considered torture?

At the beginning of the Palestinian *intifada* in January 1988, on a visit to a newly established detention center in the West Bank (Dahaniya), I saw that Palestinians suspected of involvement in minor terrorist offenses (primarily rock throwing, participating in demonstrations, etc.) were forced to stand outside in the cold while awaiting interrogation. The effort, it seemed, was aimed at "softening" the detainee to encourage cooperation with the interrogator. While not torture, the measure clearly caused discomfort, for the weather was inclement and the detainees were insufficiently attired. On the other hand, if the detainee was particularly susceptible to cold or if he had recently been sick, then the measure could be defined as causing pain. However, does that pain translate into *severe mental and physical anguish?*

Certain interrogation methods are devoid of cultural relativism because they are universal in the pain they cause. Forcing a parent to watch a child violated or spouse raped is akin to waterboarding. The anguish and utter helplessness experienced by the viewer is literally unimaginable. Since members of all cultures would consider the threat of violence against family to be emotional torture, should we define torture as only that which hurts everyone equally?

---

9. Jane Roh, "*Newsweek* Retracts Koran-Desecration Story," Fox News, May 17, 2005, *available at* http://www.foxnews.com/story/0,2933,156612,00.html/.

G. WHY TORTURE?

Why would a regime train and direct an interrogator to torture a detainee? Does the regime genuinely believe that by imposing the methods discussed above the detainee will provide actionable intelligence? While it is true that the detainee *may* provide information, there is no guarantee that he will provide actionable, viable information. There are three bases for torture: sadistic, "new sheriff in town," and interrogation-based. While all three are illegal, immoral, and do not lead to actionable intelligence, it is important to distinguish between them. Sadistic torture is just that—torture intended to satisfy the sadistic needs or tendencies of the interrogator. Historical examples abound of such measures that were not intended to contribute to prevention or punishment, but rather were very limited in their purpose.

The "new sheriff" theory suggests that when a regime assumes power it needs to send a message to various audiences. Potential audiences range from political opponents of the state to criminal elements to various groups that have raised the regime's suspicions. In order to ensure that the population not engage in political or terrorist activity, various messages can be utilized to ensure (or at least seek) passivity. While more "understandable" than sadistic torture, in that it has a pragmatic purpose (regime security), it is equally in violation of the law.

What of interrogation-based torture? While theoretically most relevant to counterterrorism, methods such as waterboarding are still illegal, immoral, and do not lead to actionable intelligence. Khalid Sheikh Mohammed, who took credit for more than 30 terrorist operations (including personally beheading reporter Daniel Pearl and masterminding the 9/11 attacks), claimed that he was tortured by the CIA before his confession.

If Mohammed's confession was the result of waterboarding, the risks to civil democratic society outweigh the benefits. Democratic regimes that torture detainees — who are no more than suspects — approach a "slippery slope" that endangers the core values of civil society. Are core values more important than survival? That is, do democratic values outweigh government's primary responsibility to protect the public? Does the post-9/11 world require different methods and approaches?

If the principle of the "limits of power" is to be applied, then the state cannot train nor direct its interrogators to torture. In the discussion regarding the limits of power, there is no word more dangerous than "exception." The concept of exceptions in the torture context is nothing more than a pretext to engage in severe violations of civil and human rights. Prevention of dramatic terrorist events through torture is so overwhelmingly slim that it does not justify engaging in excessive interrogation that would ultimately destroy the essence of democratic states.

On the other hand, states must protect themselves and interrogation methods within reason must be implemented. Analyzing interrogation is significantly enhanced by addressing it from the perspective of three audiences: interrogators, the public, and the legal-judicial infrastructure.

1. Interrogators

Interrogators have repeatedly stated that interrogation is a matter of asserting control over the detainee. To do so requires gaining the trust and confidence of that individual. According to interrogators, psychological methods are much more effective than physical means. Nevertheless, there is little doubt that the latter are critical to the process. The question is one of degree. Standing outside in the cold would be considered a means to "soften" the detainee prior to interrogation. Interrogators claim that imposition of physical measures (within limits) establishes control.

Control, however, is lost when the interrogator slaps or hits the detainee. Then the latter knows that the former has reached the point of frustration and has lost professional detachment. While professional detachment is irrelevant in the sadistic or "new sheriff" paradigm, it is critical to the interrogation-based regime. If the ultimate desire is to get *correct* information, as opposed to *any* information, then how the interrogator conducts the interrogation is crucial. Interrogators charged with gathering actionable information must restrain themselves.

Receiving misinformation or disinformation from a detainee is quantifiably worse than not receiving any information. The intelligence and operational community will be prone to act on information received and may "send the cavalry." However, if the information received (as a result of illegal means) was incorrect, than the "cavalry" will be sent to where the bomb is *not* located. Conversely, if the interrogator were to apply lawful means, the possibility of receiving correct information increases exponentially.

Psychological means are legitimate in an effort to gain a detainee's trust. But there is a limit—moral and legal—with respect to non-physical measures. Threatening a detainee that unless he confesses, his wife and daughter will be arrested and sexually violated is akin to striking the detainee himself, if not worse. Humiliating and degrading the detainee (without physical contact) as a psychological means is commonly applied. Its legality depends on limits; degrading the detainee (even if devoid of physical contact) is, according to interrogators, an ineffective tool.

Certain coercive interrogation measures are lawful, provided they are subject to strict control and oversight. Those measures are:

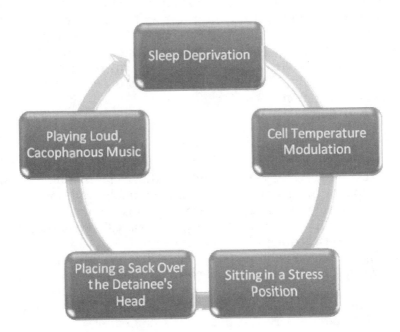

These measures, while certainly not controversy-free, reflect a balancing act between traditional criminal law interrogation (lawful) and torture (unlawful). However, their implementation is predicated on the following safeguards and controls:

Written authorization from the head of Security or Intelligence Services required before implementing any of the measures

Responsibility and accountability for harm that may befall the detainee is assumed by the Head of Security of Intelligence Service

A licensed physician must be physically present at the detention center 24 hours a day

The licensed physician must be subject to the Hippocratic oath and therefore have a patient-physician relationship with the detainee. The physician must not be in the chain of command

Application of the measures is subject to strict time limits

In seeking to develop a balanced approach to interrogation, the overarching purpose is to enable interrogators to get the much-needed information, while not violating the detainee's rights. The coercive interrogation regime is not "torture lite"; neither is it a conversation with a "cup of tea and biscuit." It reflects the limits of intelligence-gathering while seeking to gather relevant operational information. While not a perfect process, it addresses many of the concerns raised both by interrogators regarding limits and by human rights organizations regarding excess in interrogations.

2. The Public

In response to a terrorist attack, the public's reaction is usually a "call for blood." While perhaps understandable, that call can result in tragedy. It is the role of the executive to restrain the public and not engage in excess that, once unleashed, can become a runaway train. The public's call for excess can lead to "by all means necessary," "whatever it takes," and "they don't need rights" mentalities.

If responding to a public outcry, then rather than systematically interrogating suspects subject to a rights-based regime (including the possibility of adopting the coercive interrogation model), interrogators will apply measures more commonly associated with sadistic or "new sheriff" paradigms. This does not serve the public for a number of reasons:

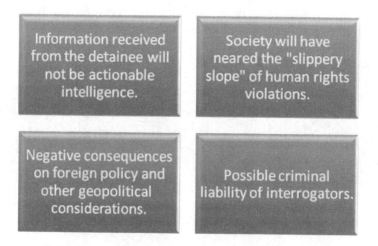

Judges ruling on the admissibility of a confession must carefully examine a wide range of factors. In a civil democratic regime, the trial can proceed only if the defendant confessed of his or her own free will and volition. While government may respond to the public's demands, judges and prosecutors alike have a legal obligation to uphold the law.

3. Legal-Judicial Infrastructure

In the "he said, she said" paradigm that reflects the interrogation process, judges and prosecutors must be extraordinarily scrupulous, particularly in the immediate aftermath of a terrorist attack. Otherwise, the judiciary and legal process are complicit in potential violations of human rights.

In cases brought before me, the uncertainty regarding the voluntariness of the defendant's confession was the primary issue. Seeking to understand why someone would confess to a crime is a major challenge facing members of the bench. The advantage of a mini-trial is that it forces the judiciary to adopt a hands-on approach regarding the interrogation regime. The same holds true for prosecutors who must analyze, with a critical and discerning eye, the viability and validity of the confession brought before them.

In doing so, the unknowns are more pronounced than the knowns. However, a decision must be made by those who were not there. That is a point of extraordinary importance for the decision maker who is entering the fray with a major handicap. What facilitates the process is the denunciation of torture (including "torture-lite") and the adoption—*in writing*—of clearly articulated limits of interrogation.

CHAPTER 8

STATE-SPONSORED TERRORISM

A. INTRODUCTION

The relationship between states — and only states — was the bedrock of international law and stability in the traditional world order. In the post-9/11 world, however, concepts, terminology, and relationships that once had been the norm have been fundamentally challenged, if not completely changed. In this new world order, non-state actors have become as capable of exacting change in international relations and domestic politics as an actual nation-state. These non-state actors present a unique challenge in the field of counterterrorism.

A non-state actor is any individual acting on behalf of any organization that is not a state. Such organizations may range from the United Way to Catholic Relief to al-Qaeda. The term "non-state actor" is as broad as the inseparable gulf between one organization dedicated to charity, the other to death and destruction. Understanding the concept of the non-state actor requires us to examine the status of the individual non-state actor and to examine the question of support — if any — for that actor. Defining "non-state actors," as well as defining the rights and obligations of states and individuals supporting these actors, is critical in counterterrorism.

When individuals are convicted of membership in terrorist organizations — Hamas in Israel, Shining Path in Peru, the IRA in Northern Ireland — they are considered members acting on behalf of that organization. These organizations are separate and distinct from a state entity. The Hamas member is not acting on behalf of the State of Palestine (which does not exist); the Shining Path member is inherently challenging Peru; and the IRA member sought to defeat the British military in Ireland. The focus of all three is action on behalf of an organization whose goal is defeating the state relevant to their circumstances. For them, membership in an organization is an integral, if not crucial, element of their actions.

But membership in what? If the terrorist non-state actor is not acting on behalf of a state, on whose behalf are they acting? A non-state entity, such as al-Qaeda? A non-state entity supported by a nation-state? For example, Hezbollah is considered by many to be acting on behalf of Iran, who supplies the Lebanese-based group through Syria, which acts as a conduit.

QUESTIONS TO CONSIDER

1. Who stands to gain what from the state-sponsorship relationship?
2. Whose interests are at stake?
3. Who "calls the shots"?
4. What rights and obligations does the state sponsor incur? What are the righs of the attacked state with respect to the sponsoring state?
5. Against whom does the principle of self-defense (whether articulated in accordance with the *Caroline* Doctrine, Article 51 of the UN Charter, or additional theories) apply: the non-state actor, the state sponsor, or the proxy?
6. Does a sponsoring state release the non-state actor from international law obligations? Does the sponsoring state assume these obligations and consequences instead?
7. Should a non-state actor acting on behalf of a state be considered "as if" a state?
8. What is the relationship between the supporting and proxy states, and what are the rights of the attacked state to both?

B. INDEPENDENCE

In discussing non-state actors, one of the important issues to discuss is the degree of their independence. How dependent are they on outside sources for means (arms, money), support (political, moral), and logistics (training, medical care)? Organizations can range from being highly independent, able to provide their own means, support and logistics, to highly dependent, relying on a state to provide almost all of these things.

HIGHLY INDEPENDENT	SEMI-INDEPENDENT	DEPENDENT
Al-Qaeda	Hamas, Shining Path, IRA	Hezbollah (relies on Iran)

In what way might an organization become dependent upon outside sources? The IRA was dependent upon financial contributions from individuals; Hamas is dependent upon Islamic charities; Sadaam Hussein, prior to his downfall, financially rewarded the families of suicide bombers; Hezbollah is dependent on Iran for financing and arms, and Syria as a conduit for Iranian-provided arms. Furthermore, is a non-state actor more or less dangerous once it has become dependent upon a state? Highly independent non-state actors like al-Qaeda are able to call their own shots and are not accountable to constituencies or critics. This might lead one to believe that dependent non-state actors are unable to exact the same damage as another group. Yet the key difference is that when a non-state actor is supported by a nation-state, the attacked state (victim) may have limited options regarding against whom to respond. To illustrate, we will examine the relationship between non-state actors such as Hezbollah and their patrons.

C. HOW DO STATES RESPOND TO STATE-SPONSORED TERRORISM?

When terrorist organizations are dependent on states for support, it is appropriate to view the relationship as a three-category model:

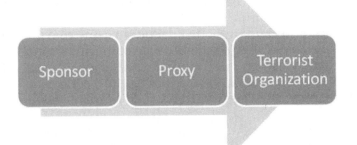

Sponsor   Proxy   Terrorist Organization

Hezbollah is a terrorist organization that receives financial support from Iran, the sponsor. But in order to effectively conduct attacks against Israel, Hezbollah must be based in Lebanon. Furthermore, both Hezbollah and Iran depend on Syria, which provides logistical support by allowing transfer of arms from Iran to Hezbollah and the establishment of terrorist bases in Syria. In this model, Syria and Lebanon are proxy states, though with arguably different levels of culpability. Syria's proxy role is an active one — Lebanon's ranges from passive to unwilling, as for one reason or another, it will not or cannot stop Hezbollah from using its territory as a base.

If counterterrorism is just that—countering terrorism—then the key question in addressing state-sponsored terrorism is, "Against whom is the state protecting itself?" The non-state actor? The sponsoring state? Proxies that the sponsoring state employs? In developing viable, effective and legal counterterrorism policy, national leaders are obligated to differentiate between categories—one response does not fit all. In doing so, the critical questions are as follows:

- What is the threat the state faces?
- Who is responsible for the threat?
- How imminent is the threat?
- What is the most effective, legal and efficient manner to neutralize the threat?

1. The Bush Doctrine

President Bush's National Security Strategy (Oct. 2002) articulated a clear, proactive policy with respect to nation's supporting terrorism:

1. America will hold to account nations that are compromised by terror, including those who harbor terrorists—because the allies of terror are the enemies of civilization. The United States and countries cooperating with us must not allow the terrorists to develop new home bases. Together, we will seek to deny them sanctuary at every turn.
2. We will cooperate with other nations to deny, contain and curtain our enemies' efforts to acquire dangerous technologies.... And, as a matter of common sense and self-defense, America will act against such emerging threats before they are fully formed.... In the new world we have entered, the only path to peace and security is the path of action.
3. We will make no distinction between terrorists and those who knowingly harbor or provide aid to them.
4. We will not hesitate to act alone, if necessary, to exercise our right of self-defense by acting preemptively against such terrorists, to prevent them from doing harm against our people.
5. For centuries, international law recognized that nations need not suffer an attack before they can lawfully take action to defend themselves against forces that present an imminent danger of attack. Legal scholars and international jurists often conditioned the legitimacy of preemption on the existence of an imminent threat.... We must adapt the concept of imminent threat to the capabilities and objectives of

today's adversaries.... The United States has long maintained the option of preemptive actions to counter a sufficient threat to our national security.... To forestall or prevent such hostile acts by our adversaries, the United States will, if necessary, act preemptively.... The United States cannot remain idle while dangers gather.[1]

State sponsorship of terrorism, whether direct or indirect, is not a new phenomenon—the PLO benefited from Soviet training and support. What is new in the aftermath of 9/11 is the determination by policy makers to define state sponsors of terrorism as *direct threats* to the nation-state itself, rather than tangential problems requiring diplomatic solutions. Operational counterterrorism has been expanded beyond the terrorist who kills Australian revelers in a Bali disco to include those giving support and refuge to the terror organization.

But is this a positive development for counterterrorism? By articulating a policy suggesting that state sponsors of terrorism present a direct threat to the targeted state, we may have stretched the concept of self-defense beyond the point of recognition. If so, does it even make sense to frame the argument in terms of international law's definition of "self-defense" when responding to state-supported terrorism? Furthermore, decision makers must consider the implications of stretching the bounds of self-defense. The Bush Doctrine seems to imply that a sovereign nation is "attackable" whenever it provides support to a terrorist organization. How much support is required before the state meets the threshold of attackability?

It is unclear at this venture what the doctrine genuinely suggests. To date, the U.S. has implemented the Bush Doctrine once—the invasion of Afghanistan. When the U.S. attacked Afghanistan, the decision was predicated on support the Taliban provided al-Qaeda. The Administration was careful to distinguish between the Taliban (a regime recognized by only three countries as the legitimate Afghan government) and Afghanistan itself, in particular its citizens.

Similarly, Israel has attacked terrorist organization training sites located in sovereign nations. Following a 2003 suicide bombing in Haifa that killed 19 people, the Israeli Air Force attacked a terrorist training camp in Syria. Syria immediately protested to the international community, but Israel claimed that Syrian airspace was not violated because the target was the camp, not Syria proper. Yet these distinctions are illusory. The reality is if Israel were to have said that the target was Syria and that Syrian air space had been violated (which it *was*, denial aside), then Israel could be accused of an act of war against Syria. The

---

1. National Security Strategy, as cited in Guiora, Amos N., *Global Perspectives on Legislative and Policy Responses to Terrorism* 7 SDJIL 1 (2005).

Israeli denial reflected a clear desire to avoid escalation with Syria while sending a message to the terrorists.

Practical realities often dictate how states respond to state-sponsored terrorism. During the course of the Israel-Hezbollah war in the summer of 2006, Israel's military effort was directed at Hezbollah targets in Southern Lebanon. Yet it was widely known that Iran was Hezbollah's primary, if not exclusive, supplier of finances and armaments. Israel's actions had significant geopolitical ramifications, but it must be acknowledged that is efforts were primarily tactical, or short-term, rather than strategic. Had Israeli decision makers been intent on attacking terrorism at its core, striking Iran itself would have better illustrated that policy. Geopolitics made attacking Iran a practical impossibility for Israel.

2. Who Are State Sponsors of Terrorism?

In the United States, the Secretary of State determines when a state is declared a "sponsor" of terrorism. When the Secretary declares that a state is guilty of repeatedly supporting acts of international terrorism, there are four main categories of sanctions the U.S. can level against it: restrictions on U.S. foreign assistance, a ban on defense exports and sales, controls over exports, and miscellaneous financial and other restrictions. Such a designation also results in penalties for persons and countries who engage in certain types of trade with state sponsors.[2]

Currently, the U.S. has designated five countries as state sponsors of terrorism.

1. Cuba — designated March 1, 1982
2. Iran — designated January 19, 1984
3. North Korea — designated January 20, 1988
4. Sudan — designated August 12, 1993
5. Syria — designated December 29, 1979

3. How to Engage Sponsors, Proxies, and Sponsored Terror Groups Effectively

Defining effectiveness in the counterterrorism paradigm is a matter of much disagreement, if not controversy. The following definition is offered:

> Operational counterterrorism is effective if the terrorist infrastructure suffers serious damage, thereby preventing a particular, planned attack from going forth and postponing or impacting plans for future attacks.

---

2. State Sponsors of Terrorism, U.S. Department of State, available at http://www.state.gov/s/ct/c14151.htm/.

If Iran is Hezbollah's sponsor and Syria is a conduit between the two, Israel's goals of significantly damaging Hezbollah would have been most effectively met had the Israeli Air Force (IAF) attacked Iranian targets or Syrian infrastructure, thereby impeding the shipment of military material from Iran to Lebanon. Under traditional notions of international law, could Israel not make a self-defense argument for attacking Iran and/or Syria? Does legitimate self-defense not include attacking targets of the enabling nation-state?

D. THE LEGITIMACY OF RESPONDING TO SPONSORS AND PROXIES MILITARILY

The status of the proxy nation (the conduit for arms) raises an additional, possible target in the context of operational counterterrorism. Perhaps an easier issue than the sponsor, the proxy is just that—the proxy doing the primary sponsor's bidding. As the proxy is generally the weaker of the two nation-states (implicit in its largely subservient role), it makes for a more inviting target. But regardless of how convenient a target the proxy has made itself, the question remains as to whether the proxy is a legitimate target according to international law. Does its role as a conduit for arms elevate it to the status of the sponsoring state, and can the doctrine of self-defense be applied with the same verve to the two states?

A broad interpretation of the Bush Doctrine suggests that the proxy state is as legitimate a target as the sponsoring state. "Harbor," if expansively defined, extends to the passive, including providing mere shelter. By facilitating transportation (or any other measure relevant to its proxy role), the nation-state is actively engaged in the terrorism effort carried out by a terrorist organization. If a terrorist organization would be unable to attack the nation-state's civilian targets without arms transported through the proxy state, then the doctrine of aggressive self-defense would justify military action against the proxy.

Legal considerations are but one component of the dilemma. Policy makers must also seek to gauge consequences of an attack on another nation-state—albeit one perceived as weak, or at least weaker, than the sponsoring state. In examining tactical as compared to strategic considerations, the question is whether the targeted nation-state is actually willing to militarily engage another nation-state. This is particularly the case when the impetus is the action of a third-party terrorist organization.

In addressing rights, responsibilities, and obligations of state sponsors of terrorism, the question is whether harboring (defined either expansively or narrowly) is tantamount to an act of war. The quandary is clear — while according to international law, war can only be between states, terrorism is best defined as "armed conflict short of war." The state sponsor is providing harbor to an entity (terrorist organization) that cannot be at war under the very definition of the word. However, the very act of very harboring places the sponsoring state (arguably less responsible for actual acts of terror) in the position of risking war with the threatened state.

Example

> Twenty-two civilians of Country A have just been killed and another 72 wounded following a terrorist attack in a crowded shopping center. The public is clamoring for the government to take immediate action; the media is feeding the frenzy by interviewing enraged citizens and elected officials from the opposition party.
>
> The terrorist who committed the suicide bombing is from a locally based terrorist organization (D) committed to a clearly expressed cause. Because of D's "clan-like" structure, government sources have been unable to penetrate the organization. What is known is that because of the organization's lack of resources (financial, arms), they are largely depended on foreign largesse.
>
> The organization's primary benefactor long in disagreement with the affected government is a nation state (B) with deep pockets and powerful military. Without assistance from Country B, the terrorist organization is unable to commit similar acts.
>
> In an unconvincing TV appearance, the Prime Minister of Country A urged restraint, promising that the military would take appropriate action — but dodged when asked if she would order the armed forces to strike at Country B. When asked regarding aggressive self-defense, the Prime Minister responded, "Yes, dependent on reliable and corroborated intelligence information."
>
> When presented such irrefutable evidence that Country B was bankrolling the terrorist organization, the Prime Minister sought to deflect by pointing an accusatory finger at the banking laws of Country C.

As the legal advisor charged with providing the Prime Minister of Country A in the above Example, I would recommend the following course of action:

With respect to the Terrorist Organization D:

- Detain known operatives suspected of involvement in the attack (planners, doers and those responsible for logistical support).

- Identify individuals who meet targeted killing requirement (predicated on intelligence information that they are planning additional acts of terrorism).
- "Shake the trees" regarding involvement of previously unknown individuals.
- Consider administrative sanctions against involved individuals.

With respect to Country B:

- Would recommend to the Prime Minister that military action against a state sponsor of terrorism is lawful either in response to an attack clearly sponsored by the state or in an effort to prevent a planned attack (provided a strict scrutiny of intelligence information test is implemented);
- Would recommend to the Prime Minister engaging the international community in an effort to impose sanctions and/or condemnation of Country B as a state sponsor of terrorism. To do this effectively requires gathering and presenting intelligence information while protecting sources and avoiding repetition of mistakes made by then-Secretary of State Powell when he addressed the UN regarding Iraq's nuclear weapons program;
- Would recommend directly addressing — through the media, as an example — Country B's government warning them that unless their support of terrorism cease, they are considered a legitimate target as are viewed as attacked country A.

With respect to Country C:

- Would articulate to the international community that "C" as proxy (due to lenient banking laws enabling financing of terrorism) endangers the nation's citizens and therefore are considered a legitimate target;
- Would directly (including media) or through third parties pressure "C" to amend relevant banking laws;
- Would seek international pressure for imposition of economic sanctions prior to declaring war and/or taking military measures (moving forces to a common border, ordering air "fly-bys");
- While C is a "legitimate target" akin to the sponsoring state, would be difficult to convince the international community that full military action is justifiable and meets recognized self-defense standards (*Caroline*, Article 51 and additional paradigms). Accordingly, a limited military action — perhaps against a major lending institution or the national treasury — so that there is a direct link between the cause (terror financing) and act.

What is the operational significance of state-sponsored terrorism in the post-9/11 world? The suggestion is that the definition of legitimate military targets in the counterterrorism paradigm has been broadened to include states. If, in the traditionally understood counterterrorism model, an attacked state would limit its operational response to the terror organization responsible for an attack, the new paradigm suggests the response (or prevention) reverts to a nation state conflict. This is particularly problematic because the sponsoring state has not (as traditionally understood) directly attacked the "attacked state" (A in the Example above) but rather done so through a non-state actor. The immediate significance of A attacking B in response to D's actions is the imposition of *direct responsibility* on the nation-state.

In imposing this direct responsibility, A's decision makers are faced with the following dilemma:

WHAT ARE LEGITIMATE TARGETS IN COUNTRY B?		
Relevant government institutions responsible for facilitating D's attack? For example, the Department of Defense or Security Services installations.	Country B's infrastructure — roads, bridges, airports — provided that military necessity rather than revenge against the civilian population can be demonstrated.	Military targets like tanks, planes, bases, etc.

The answer to the above question is dependent on answering another question: What is the purpose of the attack? Should A determine that B is a legitimate target, then it is required to articulate (at least to itself) the goals in attacking the sponsoring state. If the goal is revenge (though a natural human response, a clear violation of international law) then A will, in all probability, not limit its action to a specific, identified target. Rather, it will engage in an indiscriminate response, be it against innocent civilians or civilian infrastructure. Such a response, which would be viewed by the international community as disproportionate, would justify a counter-reaction by B against A's civilian population. The conflict — now a war — would very quickly escalate beyond the original, limited terror attack. Is this the inevitable result of expanding the definition of legitimate target in the context of state-supported terrorism?

E. LEGITIMACY AND EFFECTIVENESS

On the assumption (with all the inherent danger in "assuming") that neither A nor B from the example above are interested in a full-scale military conflict, then A's justifiable response is limited to military targets only. However, the action will clearly be subject to much disagreement in the international community.

Why limit targets? Not only does international law so require, but A's case in the court of international opinion will be significantly strengthened by a response limited to non-civilian targets. However, for such an attack to be effective (in this case defined as deterring B from further support of D or other terrorist organizations), the following decision must be made: Is the attack (such an aerial bombing or long-range missile) intended to kill individuals (albeit members of the military or security services) or only sending a message?

EXAMPLE

In response to the alleged Iraqi assassination plot directed against the first President Bush, then–President Clinton ordered a nighttime bombing of the Iraqi Military Intelligence headquarters. Effective? Absolutely not.

If A decides that B is a legitimate target in the context of state-supported terrorism, then the recommended action to A's decision makers is not a nighttime attack, but rather an attack on a military installation occupied by security personnel. Such an action, while "upping the ante" between the two states, also exhibits restraint and proportionality since civilians were not targeted. This is in direct contrast to the terrorist attack that predicated the response in the first place.

When requested to offer operational counterterrorism legal advice to IDF military commanders, my recommendation was—if operationally possible—to target a terrorist organization's leaders. While foot soldiers are critical, they are not the keystones to terror organizations. The essence of effective and lawful counterterrorism is directed against the planners, senders, and financiers. In targeting the leaders (equivalent to the state sponsoring terrorism in this paradigm), effectiveness requires forcefully deterring, if not actually preventing, while respecting the restraints imposed by the rule of law.

The legal advice provided always emphasized restraint—whether in response to a terrorist attack that killed five innocent individuals or one which claimed 25 lives. Translated to state-sponsored terrorism, this policy reflects a balanced policy approach against a target defined as legitimate.

In determining whether to act militarily against the proxy state, it is important to assess whether the proxy is doing its own bidding or acting under duress. While acting under duress does not free the proxy state of accountability and responsibility—it is a sovereign state, after all—this is an issue that warrants consideration prior to military engagement. While the concept of a nation state "hiding" behind another is highly problematic, it is an issue to consider, even if it contradicts the very essence of state sovereignty.

In the context of the 2006 Lebanon war, did Syria willingly serve as Iran's conduit of arms to Hezbollah? From available media reports and intelligence assessments, the overwhelming if not unanimous conclusion is that President Assad *willingly* facilitated arms movement intended for Hezbollah through Syria. A nation-state willingly acting as a conduit argu-ably falls into the category of broadly defined legitimate targets. While Syria is not the sponsor—the arms originated in Iran—its role in their transport is critical. Therefore, strategically attacking Syrian targets will hamper Hezbollah's and Iran's efforts against Israel.

What does attacking Syria mean operationally? When this issue was raised with respect to the sponsoring state, the recommendation was to attack a military instillation when personnel are present. Is the same true for the proxy state? Are the two—sponsoring and proxy—states ulti-mately equivalent legitimate targets, or is differentiation and distinction appropriate? Just as all terrorists are not the same, not all state actors supporting terrorism are the same.

Categorization and distinction are required from a policy and legal perspective alike. The proxy state occupies the middle ground between "senders" (those who send suicide bombers on their mission; for the pur-poses of this discussion similar to the "sponsor") and "doers" (the foot soldiers who commit the suicide bombing). Therefore, what are the rights and obligations of the two relevant states—proxy and attacked?

By actively enabling the passage of weapons through its sovereign territory, has Syria, as the proxy, declared war on Israel? In the terrorism paradigm, is the individual who drives the suicide bomber to the pizza parlor a terrorist to the same degree as the "doer"? Without the driver, the bomber cannot get to the site; without the proxy, the weapons cannot reach Hezbollah. If the driver is viewed with less severity than the sender ("sponsor"), then is military action appropriate against the proxy?

In the traditional international law paradigm, the answer would be negative, for the proxy has not directly declared nor initiated war against the attacked state.

However, in the context of an expanded definition of legitimate targets, can a proxy nation be upgraded to the status approaching that of the sponsor? In the scenario described above, Country C is a legitimate target since it facilitates arms transfer. It is not akin to the sponsor. Therefore, in applying a differentiation theory, the question is what operational measures are legitimate. What targets inside C can be attacked?

Civilian targets cannot be attacked; that is a basic international law obligation. Similar to legal advice offered IDF military commanders, the obligation is to specifically target those responsible and accountable for the facilitation of arms movement. In an effort to prevent arms movement, military installations or infrastructure enabling the movement are legitimate targets.

However, unlike the sponsor paradigm, the actions of the proxy do not justify military action (aerial bombing) when personnel are present. Rather, in an effort to "send a message" by upping the ante, the recommended course of action (subject to significant opposition in the court of international opinion) is (in spite of its implicit weakness) reminiscent of President Clinton's actions. As C is a proxy, message sending is appropriate—whereas in the planned assassination of President Bush, the Iraqis were the "doers." The justification for the recommendation is premised on the fact that according to available intelligence information, the Iraqis were directly responsible for the planned assassination, whereas in the present scenario C is a proxy, not the dominant actor.

Is this distinction implementable? Is this distinction effective? Is this distinction the wave of the future?

F. CONCLUSION

Sponsors, proxies, and terrorist organization all bear responsibility for their actions, but not to the same degree. President Bush's National Security Strategy expresses a very aggressive model for responding to state-sponsored terrorism. In the context of geopolitical realities, it is difficult to imagine many nation-states adopting the doctrine. Lawful and effective counterterrorism measures require *distinguishing* between actors, their circumstances, and actions—the Bush Doctrine fails on all three counts.

Similarly, the Clinton response was a tactical failure and strategic blunder. While likely lawful (in an expanded model of legitimate targets) the action was perceived by the intended audience as a sign of weakness.

Better not to respond in some cases than to do so when the result is a perception of operational incapability.

The distinction between the three categories is premised on the theory that broadening the categories of legitimate targets by an attacked state meets international law standards. However, that is tempered by the requirement to balance and differentiate between the three categories. To that end, the scenario and its analysis is recommended as the model to adopt in the age of state-sponsored terrorism.

CHAPTER 9

TERRORISM AND THE MEDIA

A. INTRODUCTION

Terrorists have a cause that they seek to advance through violence and intimidation. From the terrorist's perspective, the more people the organization can intimidate, influence, or convince, the better. The media therefore plays a key role, perhaps unwittingly, in the dynamic between terrorism and society. In reviewing major terrorist attacks of the past 40 years, the seminal event was the PLO attack on the Israeli Olympic team at the Munich Games — not because it was the first PLO attack on Israeli targets, nor necessarily the most "daring" or "flamboyant." Previous hijackings of major commercial airlines would more comfortably fall in those categories.

The basis for defining the Munich Olympic Games attack as seminal is largely in direct proportion to its "media moment." For the first time, a terror attack played out in "real time" on the world stage. Not merely limited to the deaths of 11 Israeli athletes and one German police officer, the Munich attacks in 1972 hit home as camera crews filmed the events live from the Olympic village. Those of age remember the photo of the masked terrorist on the balcony; those not of age have seen the picture too many times to count.

QUESTIONS TO CONSIDER

1. Is it a goal of terrorists to be on TV? If so, do terrorist organizations try to tailor their actions to secure public sympathy and minimize outrage?
2. Is the goal to bring awareness to a cause?
3. Is the media an unwitting tool in the hands of terrorists?
4. How does the state (if at all) use the media to its advantage?
5. Do the media (intentionally or otherwise) contribute to terrorism?

continued on next page

6. Is the state sufficiently proactive with respect to terrorism or is the initiative inherently with the terrorist?
7. Is it possible to successfully sound bite an occupation force, or is the David-Goliath paradigm unbeatable?

In discussing terrorism and the media, the questions go far beyond the lens. Questions must be asked from three different perspectives — the media, policy makers, and terrorists.

B. THE MEDIA

What is the proper role of the media in the aftermath of a terrorist attack? What is the proper role of the media in a tense political situation that includes acts of terror in the past and the likelihood of more in the future? In the American paradigm, the media is referred to as "the fourth estate" because it is expected to be a government watchdog. The Society of Professional Journalists Code of Ethics states that the "duty of the journalist is to further [public enlightenment] by seeking truth and providing a fair and comprehensive account of events and issues." What this means, however, is a matter of interpretation. There is no check on the media other than the media itself and the marketplace.

Is the media a passive actor, simply filming whatever unfolds and leaving the viewer to interpret the scenes? If the members of the media are mere observers, do they have a responsibility to accurately and fairly report both sides of a particular issue? What is the media's proper role? Many different schools of thought have emerged on this issue, some even extrapolating from ethical theorists of the past.

OBSERVER-COMMENTATOR				
Rawlsian: John Rawls proposed the idea of the "veil of ignorance." This view suggests the journalist must imagine	*Aristotelian:* Espouses moderation, coverage which is neither overtly patriotic nor indulgent toward terrorists.	*Kantian:* Asks, "To whom does the journalist owe a duty?" Also, two categorical imperatives must be	*John Stuart Mill:* Suggests journalists should seek the greatest contribution to the general welfare.	*Ida B. Wells:* Wrote that some stories involved inherently evil subject matter — lynching of African Americans in Wells'

OBSERVER-COMMENTATOR				
which rules they would want followed if they didn't know what lot in life they had drawn. Also described as "justice as fairness."		kept in mind: (1) The journalist should act as if his/her action would lead to a universal law to which all others would adhere; (2) Individuals should always be treated as an end and never as a means.		time — and therefore it was not necessary to seek out that side of the story.

All journalists purport to provide "accurate" information, but accuracy is usually defined by the journalist. If "observer" is the correct label to put on the media, then perhaps in response to the Madrid train bombing (which killed over 190 Spaniards), the media ought to merely show pictures of the carnage. Similarly, in response to Daniel Pearl's beheading, should the media as observer show the beheading acting as a mirror, simply reflecting the reality of the moment? Or, if the media is a commentator, then is what it chooses to show (and not show) tainted by the reporter's or network's political leanings or agenda?

Further complicating the issue is the increased sophistication of modern media telecommunications. With the ever-competitive rush to be the first to break a story in a world of blogs, podcasts, and websites streaming stories 24/7 comes an increased danger of reporting inaccurate information. For example, in October of 2007, Secretary of State Condoleezza Rice's motorcade was detoured during a visit to Israel and the West Bank while authorities investigated a suspicious vehicle on the Palestinian side of the border. Concerns were allayed within minutes, but during the brief stop, wire service reporters traveling with Rice alerted their editors to the delay. While the reporters also promptly informed their desks that no complications had arisen, the damage was already done. The AP alert went out at 4:39 EST on the international news wire. While the wire sent out an additional alert announcing the false alarm eight minutes later, newscasters had already begun programming breaking news banners flashing across the screen about Secretary Rice's "security concerns."[1]

How the reporter portrays — if at all — dissimilar viewpoints is the essence of the issue. If the reporter's perspective is that one side is the victim and the other is the aggressor, then how are the aggressor's citizens portrayed if their family members have just been killed in a terrorist bombing?

1. A New Vision of Media Responsibility?

In 1947, the Hutchins Commission[2] concluded that the media's power should be balanced by a commitment to social good, a concept which has been generally accepted by the media. A commitment to social good has typically been interpreted to mean "serving as a watchdog against government."[3] Yet there is more that the media can do, as articulated by the 9/11 Commission Report, which criticized journalists' performance pre-9/11. "The most important failure was one of imagination….The terrorist danger from Bin Ladin and al Qaeda was not a major topic for policy debate among the public, the media, or in Congress."[4]

Prior to 9/11, contemporary media critics including Neil Postman, Murrey Marder, Bill Kovach, and Tom Rosenstiel called for a regeneration of American journalism.[5] In *The Global Journalist: News and Conscience in a World of Conflict*, Philip Seib has argued that "as change takes place, the news media have the responsibility to capture the attention of an often

---

1. Michael Abramowitz, *False Alarm Frenzy*, WASHINGTON POST, available at http://blog.washingtonpost.com/on-the-plane/fire_alarm_frenzy.html?hpid=sec-world/.

2. The Hutchins Commission on the Freedom of the Press (commonly known as the "Hutchins Commission") was convened from 1942 to 1947. It produced a code of responsibility for the press: (1) truthful, comprehensive and intelligent account of the day's events in a context that gives them meaning; (2) provide a forum for the exchange of comment and criticism; (3) a projection of a representative picture of the constituent groups in society; (4) a presentation and clarification of the goals and values of society; (5) full access to the day's intelligence. It also provided recommendations for how the government and the public should behave to promote the freedom of the press.

3. FREDERICK S. SEIBERT ET AL., FOUR THEORIES OF THE PRESS: THE AUTHORITARIAN, LIBERTARIAN, SOCIAL RESPONSIBILITY AND SOVIET COMMUNIST CONCEPTS OF WHAT THE PRESS SHOULD BE AND DO 74 (3d ed., 1982).

4. National Commission on Terrorist Attacks Upon the United States, The 9/11 Commission Report Executive Summary 9 (2004).

5. Glen Feighery, *Watchdogs for a New War: The 9/11 Commission and Terrorism Coverage*, working draft.

disengaged public....Individual journalists have their own duties: to witness and report, and through their coverage to prod policymakers and the public to pay more attention to what is going on around them."[6]

In the post-9/11 world, the tension between the observer role and the commentator role may be best illustrated by Dennis D. Cali, who argued for a "participatory mode of reporting,"[7] and media ethicist Deni Elliot, who warns about the dangers inherent in excessive media identification.[8] Cali argues that it is appropriate to recognize human solidarity in a post-9/11 world, bringing journalists closer to the events and groups they cover. Elliot counters that independence is key, distinguishing between "nationalistic journalism" and "patriotic journalism." According to Elliot, nationalistic journalism "echoes what authorities want to say or what citizens want to hear," while patriotic journalism "keeps in mind what citizens need to know to make educated decisions for self-governance."

In *The Press*, W.L. Bennett and W. Serrin propose that the press's watchdog role should involve in-depth investigation to educate the public "on matters of importance for the working of American democracy."[9] They suggest that in recent years, the press has failed to live up to its historical roots of working in concert with social movements. Suggesting a compromise between Cali and Elliot, Bennett and Serrin suggest that journalists should collaborate with government and public-interest agents to maximize their role as watchdogs.

Perhaps, as Glen Feighery suggests, when journalists cover terrorism, they have an ethical duty to warn of potential danger.[10] Pre-9/11, there was no systematic journalistic monitoring of terrorist threats, but rather systematic coverage *after* major events occurred. As the Report pointed out, "all this reportage looked backward, describing problems satisfactorily resolved."[11] Coverage of potential attacks increased toward the end of 1999, but as the millennium passed without incident, the stories ebbed. Even following the bombing of the USS *Cole*, coverage dwindled of the overall threat terrorism posed to the United States.

As Feighery discusses in "Watchdogs for a New War," the media did not significantly cover the Hart-Rudman Commission on National

---

6. Philip M. Seib, The Global Journalist 109 (2002).

7. Dennis D. Cali, *Journalism after September 11: Unity as Moral Imperative*, 17.4 Journal of Mass Media Ethics Special Issue (2002).

8. Deni Elliot, *Terrorism, Global Journalism and the Myth of the Nation State*. 19 Journal of Mass Media Ethics 29, 30 (2004).

9. W. Lance Bennett & William Serrin in The Press 169-188 (Geneva Overholser & Kathleen Hall Jamieson eds., 2005).

10. Glen Feighery, *Watchdogs for a New War: The 9/11 Commission and Terrorism Coverage*, working draft.

11. National Commission on Terrorist Attacks Upon the United States, The 9/11 Commission Report Executive Summary 360 (2004).

Security, which released its report on January 31, 2001. The Commission predicted that the U.S. was vulnerable to terrorism and recommended massive overhaul of intelligence and national defense, otherwise "Americans will likely die on American soil, possibly in large numbers." CNN, *The Los Angeles Times*, and *The Boston Globe* reported on this conclusion, but it appeared less conspicuously in *USA Today* and *The Washington Post*; the major broadcast networks, *The New York Times*, and *The Wall Street Journal* ignored it completely.[12] Citizens who relied solely on such sources for news were completely unaware that terrorism was a concern; it appears many of the U.S.'s "watchdogs" were asleep.

2. Post-9/11 Coverage

Has the press "stepped up to the plate" in the years since 9/11? Trudy Lieberman argued in the *Columbia Journalism Review* that "over the last couple of years, coverage of the effort to prevent another 9/11 has been spotty, episodic, reactive and shallow."[13] Robert Jensen has argued that "the performance of the U.S. corporate commercial news media after 9/11 has been the most profound and dangerous failure of journalism in my lifetime."[14] Yet this is not a total condemnation of the press. Throughout American history, journalism has gone through periods of reformation. The corporate nature of many journalistic outlets currently dictates cost-cutting, but popular demand from the public for a more vigorous press could lead to greater commercial support.

It is important to note that more in-depth coverage of such issues can be dangerous — one only need recall Daniel Pearl's fate, as well as the 118 journalists killed in Iraq as of October 2007. But, as Feighery argues, journalists should be expected to understand the history and geopolitics of terrorism, as well as the functions of different intelligence, military, and law-enforcement agencies. This would enable them to ask incisive and imaginative questions from a wide variety of sources inside and outside of government. Most importantly, journalists must look forward to what *might* happen — not merely backward to what has already occurred.

---

12. Glen Feighery, *Watchdogs for a New War: The 9/11 Commission and Terrorism Coverage*, working draft.

13. Trudy Lieberman. *Homeland Security: What We Don't Know Can Hurt Us*, Columbia Journalism Review (2004), *available at* http://cjrarchives.org/issues/2004/5/lieberman-homeland.asp/.

14. Robert Jensen, *"Fahrenheit 9/11" For Grown-Ups*, September 17, 2004, *available at* http://www.tompaine.com/articles/fahrenheit_911_for_grownups.php/.

C. POLICY MAKERS

With the outbreak of the Palestinian *intifada* in December 1987, I was asked to serve as the West Bank representative of the IDF JAG Corps to the foreign media. While not new to media relations (having worked in Congress for two years), the issues posed above became my roadmap. Occasionally they were my landmine. In numerous interviews and background briefings, my overwhelming sense was that explaining operational counterterrorism poses enormous challenges because many members of the foreign media instinctively viewed the terrorists as the victims.

This chapter is not intended to bash the media, but the fact is many members of the fourth estate have approached the story from the perspective of Palestinian victimology. The narrative that has often been depicted is that Palestinians are victims of Israeli occupation and therefore terrorism, in an effort to end the occupation, is legitimate.

Therein lies a key issue to consider when analyzing terrorism and the media: Who is the victim and how is the story portrayed? Former IDF Chief-of-Staff Moshe (Bugi) Ayalon described the tension as "a battle of narratives."[15] Battle is a powerful term; it conjures up images of armed conflict. Nevertheless the term is appropriate; in many ways, the fight over the media is a battle. To score points with the media (and the public it seeks to "inform" — a problematic term in itself) both sides engage in "spin" that has tactical as well as strategic implications.

A unique aspect of the military-media dynamic is the fact that in many circumstances, commanders are not given permission to talk about certain issues. A terrorist can take advantage of this — while most standards of journalist ethics demand that both sides of a story be sought out, a "no comment" from one side will usually suffice. If commanders are silent, terrorists are more than happy to fill the void with their narrative.

Even when the media is not explicitly or subconsciously painting the terrorists as victims, they may inadvertently contribute to the terrorists' cause. Dennis Pluchinsky, a senior intelligence analyst in the U.S. Department of State, accused the media of "lacking common sense" in a 2002 *Washington Post* column.[16] While the press is undoubtedly made up of intelligent and ethical professionals, as Raphael Cohen-Almagor argues, the media often does not have the same long-term view or goals that policy makers have.

Cohen-Almagor cited the example of the Iranian hostage situation from 1979-1980 when NBC broadcast a report, despite government

---

15. In a closed talk to officers of the IDF JAG Corps; the author was in attendance.
16. Dennis Pluchinsky, *Why Do Media Unwittingly Help Terrorists?*, WASHINGTON POST, June 30, 2002.

objections, that two U.S. emissaries were being dispatched to Iran. Shortly thereafter, Ayatollah Khomeini announced that the emissaries would not be received. Cohen-Almagor posits the question whether "members of the media understood the difficult position they put President Carter in when they repeatedly dwelled on the suffering of the hostages and their families, or when they pressed the president for action." Cohen-Almagor adds that the press compounds the problem by "reporting new developments and rekindling a story *that for the moment has not changed*" (emphasis added).[17]

The relationship between the press and policy makers can have negative repercussions for victims of terrorism. Cohen-Almagor provides several such examples: in 1974, terrorists took over part of a courthouse in Washington, D.C. The hostages were kept in a room, which, unbeknownst to the terrorists, contained a two-way mirror. The police were able to watch the terrorists and hostages from an adjoining room until their advantage was revealed to the public—and the terrorists—by the media. The terrorists immediately ordered their hostages to tape newspapers over the mirror.

Obviously the media does not always contribute to a dangerous situation. On 9/11, the mainstream media was able to effectively diffuse false rumors that were spreading rapidly on the Internet. But the fact remains—situations have (and likely will in the future) arise where the media either knowingly or unwittingly frustrates a state's counterterrorism methods.

D. TERRORISTS

Without instant media coverage, terrorist attacks potentially lose their impact. The attacks which are the means by which terrorists effectuate their twin goals of killing civilians and/or intimidating the civilian population, are dependent on immediate, dramatic visuals.

How do terrorists use the media? Many scholars have noted that media-oriented terrorism is the norm. Gabriel Weimann suggests "modern terrorism can be understood in terms of the production requirements of theatrical engagements."[18] By designing the attack so it reaches large audiences, terrorists can increase an attack's impact through the media.

---

17. Raphael Cohen-Almagor, *Media Coverage of Acts of Terrorism: Troubling Episodes and Suggested Guidelines*, 30 CANADIAN JOURNAL OF COMMUNICATION, available at http://www.cjc-online.ca/index.php/journal/article/viewArticle/1579/1734 (2005).

18. Gabriel Weimann, *The Theater of Terror: The Psychology of Terrorism & the Mass Media*, 9 JOURNAL OF AGGRESSION, MALTREATMENT AND TRAUMA 379 (2004).

Merely getting your picture in the paper, however, does not necessarily imply that a particular attack was effective. There is a need to address effectiveness from the terrorist perspective; doing so requires a two-pronged approach: short-term (tactical) and long-term (strategic). In examining the different approaches taken by terrorist organizations, it is important to remember that different groups have different goals. Differing goals lead to contrasting terrorist attacks, which contribute to dissimilar media relations. In addition, different goals also suggest disparate audiences that require messages be honed to specific groups.

One of the most important operative questions is whether attacking innocent civilians "advances" the cause. The question is asked not from a political perspective, but from the visual. Are pictures of dead women and children killed while eating pizza beneficial to a terrorist organization? In large part the answer depends on "who is the audience" and "what is the narrative." It is equally important to consider how the state will portray the attack and how it will respond.

Terrorist organizations have long debated who is a legitimate target. Intimidation of the innocent civilian population is an important element of the terrorism definition proposed in this book. To that end, attacking pizza parlors is not only legitimate, but advances the cause.

But does it? Do the inevitable pictures continuously and dramatically flashed on TV screens worldwide assist terrorist organizations? The answer depends on the audience. There are a number of recommended audiences to consider:

- The organization's core supporters
- Potential recruits
- The impacted citizens
- The court of international opinion

1. Core Supporters

According to experts, it is necessary to carry out terrorist attacks in order to guarantee continued support from core supporters. The core constituency will not support passive terrorism; engaging the enemy is critical to ensuring continued support from the relevant community. Media attention significantly contributes, as scenes of carnage are readily available, be it on TV, the Internet (websites, blogs), or cell phone cameras. With the media constantly feeding images to a worldwide audience, the horror of a terrorist attack can be easily and quickly regenerated.

If core supporters demand regular attacks, the terrorist organization is faced with a dilemma—too many attacks will potentially sway the court of international opinion and possibly turn off potential recruits. If the terrorist group wishes to maintain the victim role in the battle of narratives, it cannot appear too powerful or violent to outside viewers. Yet core supporters demand strong, consistent action.

Media saturation relieves this dilemma for the terrorist. One spectacular attack can—and will—be replayed over and over in images and footage on the television news, print journalism, Internet websites, and blogs. In essence, the media allows the terrorist organization to get "more bang for their buck"—and at the same time, avoid much of the vilification in the battle of narratives were they to conduct additional attacks.

While traditional corporate media might be able to recognize this phenomenon and take steps to address it, the generally unregulated Internet media will not. The traditional news media has been supplanted—if not entirely replaced—by the Internet and other fast-paced technological breakthroughs. The Internet has proven particularly successful in ensuring unlimited distribution of pictures that the mainstream media would not air.

Perhaps the best examples are the beheadings in Iraq and Pakistan of Western targets—Daniel Pearl, Nicholas Berg, Kenneth Bigley, Jack Hensley, and Eugene Armstrong. What the BBC chose not to air, the Internet readily provided. To what purpose? Obviously to satisfy morbid curiosity; but just as important was the video's "marketing" method by al-Qaeda and its supporters. Few images are more effective from that perspective than the beheading of Daniel Pearl, whose last recorded words were "I am a Jew."

2. Potential Recruits

With respect to potential recruits or "swayables," there is little doubt that the pictures referred to above are extremely effective. To an individual debating whether to join a terrorist organization, there are few recruiting posters more effective than Pearl's beheading.

Thomas Friedman discusses the frustration of disenfranchised youth in *The World Is Flat*:

> It has always been my view that terrorism is not spawned by the poverty of money. It is spawned by *the poverty of dignity*…too many good decent people [in certain parts of the world] feel the same frustration and tinge of humiliation that many of their enraged youth do. And there is a certain respect for the way these violent youth have been ready to stand up to the world and to their own leaders and defend the honor of their civilization.[19]

---

19. Thomas Friedman, The World Is Flat 400 (2005).

When photographs and video of the Daniel Pearl beheading were seen by a worldwide audience, the terrorist's power is broadcast. Potential recruits and even merely passive supporters can respect the power they themselves lack. From the perspective of the relationship between the media and terrorism, pictures are powerful motivators for future recruits. Therefore, the media not only is a vehicle for updating existing membership with respect to activities, but also for reaching out to potential membership.

3. Impacted Citizens

Terrorism seeks to kill the states' innocent civilians, yet terrorists seek to have themselves portrayed sympathetically by the media to a grieving nation. How is this task accomplished? The answer is complicated and is predicated on the organization's goal(s).

As an example: Hamas' suicide bombings in the fall of 2000 were intended to convince the Israeli public to pressure the government to withdraw from the Gaza Strip and the West Bank. By forcing the media to repeatedly film pictures of dead and injured innocent civilians, terrorists hoped the media would convey a message of "fatigue" from and "opposition" to the Israeli occupation of the West Bank and Gaza Strip. The sublime message was that if Israel were to withdraw from the areas in question, suicide bombings would cease.

The messenger was the media. In seeking to affect government policy through public pressure, Hamas identified the media as an effective transmitter of that message. Were reporters, editors, and photographers "witting" emissaries or did the narrative reflect their perspective? Re-phrased, the question is whether suicide bombings were portrayed as a self-fulfilling prophecy: as long as Israel continues to occupy the Gaza Strip and the West Bank, the bombings are inevitable. However, that is only one side of the coin — what is lost is the possibility that terrorism would occur regardless of whether Israel occupies the West Bank and the Gaza Strip.

Herein lies the rub in reporting terrorism: Are reporters expected to educate the public with respect to a wide array of issues including history, culture, religion, and politics — or are the pictures to speak for themselves? In my innumerable interviews with members of the media (Israeli and foreign alike), I would always seek to emphasize the story behind the picture.

Easier said than done. The picture — whether of a soldier misconducting at a checkpoint or the after-effects of a suicide bombing — would be far more powerful images than any words uttered by the spin masters. It was as if the picture was the spin and any effort to suggest a nuanced approach or analysis was overwhelmed by the spectacular.

As that is the reality, terrorists and counterterrorists alike must tailor their messages accordingly. The underdog (victim) will inevitably have the upper hand. My numerous efforts to explain were enormously complicated and challenged by yet another picture of Palestinian victimology. Pointing out that Israelis (Jews and Arabs alike) were victims of suicide bombing did not have the same gravitas. That is a reality decision makers must address in planning how to most effectively spin counterterrorism to the media. If the media is unquestioning and chooses to accept at face value what terrorist leaders articulate regarding motivations, goals, and methods then the media is truly nothing more than a conduit, incapable or unwilling to act as a filter.

4. International Opinion

How does all this impact the court of international opinion and to whom—if anyone—does the media owe fairness? That inevitably requires defining "fairness," which is almost an indefinable term, as terrorism is the most subjective of issues, largely defying objective analysis.

By definition, terror groups have a goal or goals they are trying to effectuate. Garnering sympathy from the international community can help the group achieve those goals. Yasser Arafat arguably understood this better than anyone—Thomas Friedman called him "the Ronald Reagan of Palestinian politics."[20] Under Arafat's leadership, the PLO fought on the world stage, with terror attacks and traditional political maneuvering alike. Arafat addressed the U.N., conducted an interview with *Playboy Magazine*, and received the Nobel Peace Prize. Time will only tell if Arafat's skill at international public relations will contribute to the establishment of a Palestinian state.

E. CONCLUSION

In examining the relationship between terrorism and the media from the perspective of the four identified target audiences, the question is what effect does coverage of a particular attack have. Examining specific incidents in the context of those audiences and measuring their effect from tactical and strategic perspectives facilitates discussion. The effectiveness quotient is predicated on absolute dichotomies—what is considered effective from the terrorist perspective is ineffective from the state's perspective and vice versa.

---

20. Thomas Friedman, From Beirut to Jerusalem 107 (1989).

Between the two extremes are the affected civilian populations (including members of the intended target audience, as well as civilians from the terrorists' community who are sometimes indirect victims of terrorism and counterterrorism alike) and the court of international opinion. The example below neatly summarizes the multiple tensions this chapter seeks to address.

EXAMPLE: BESLAN SCHOOLHOUSE ATTACK

On September 1, 2004, a group of Chechen separatists took more than 1,200 children and adults hostage in a schoolhouse in Beslan. The hostages were crowded into the school gym, denied food and water, and terrorized with homemade bombs strung from the basketball hoops overhead. On the third day of the standoff, the bombs detonated and Russian forces stormed the school. The siege resulted in the deaths of 331 people, more than half of them children.

Core supporters: The need to keep up constant attacks to ensure support for the Chechen separatist movement was certainly met with this attack. In 2002, 130 people were killed in a Moscow theater attack. In the weeks prior to the schoolhouse attack, various attacks took place in Chechnya, two airliners were bombed, and a suicide bomber attacked a Moscow subway station.

Potential recruits: After the attacks, President Putin admitted that Russia had become vulnerable to attacks from both within and without, and vowed strong new security measures, but many citizens remained skeptical.

Impacted citizens: The Russian newspaper *Izvestia* just carried a giant photo of a man holding a wounded child on its front page after the attacks.[21] *New York Times* reporter Seth Mydans described the spirit in Moscow after Beslan in almost nihilistic terms, quoting a Russian Orthodox priest as saying, "We ride on the subway and think it is for the last time. We gather in church and think it is our last liturgy."[22]

International opinion: On the first day of the standoff, the U.N. Security Council convened and demanded "the immediate and unconditional release of all hostages." President George W. Bush offered "support in any form" to Russia.

---

21. September 4, 2004 issue of *Izvestia*, pg. 1.
22. Seth Mydans, *Moscow's Gloom Deepens as Fear Becomes Routine*, N.Y. TIMES, September 5, 2004.

As traditional media—newspapers and broadcast—become more shallow in their reporting due to commercial pressures, different forms of communication (documentaries, non-fiction books) are needed to understand the complicated world in which we live. While media coverage of the Beslan attack and its aftermath has significantly dropped off in the international media, a 2005 HBO documentary called *Children of Beslan* interviewed the young survivors, who made both tragic (a boy recalls fantasizing that Harry Potter would save him: "I remembered that he had a cloak that made him invisible, and he would come and wrap me up in it, and we'd be invisible, and we'd escape") and chilling (a boy who calmly declares, "My greatest desire is to go to Chechnya and kill all those terrorists, to avenge my dad") comments.[23]

In presenting the story, the media can adopt either the role of observer (neutral) or commentator (portraying the event from the perspective of a particular political agenda). If neutral, then the camera speaks—though it is important to note that the term "objective reporting" is problematic because ultimately the viewer only sees what the camera "shows" him.

That is to say, the visual is limited to what the cameraman or reporter has chosen to show. With respect to agenda based reporting—the reporter or producer seeks to present the story from a particular slant and will, to that end, either gloss over inconvenient facts or choose not to show current events from the other side. In the "twenty second sound bite" culture, it is all but impossible to address historical issues from the two perspectives (competing); it is far easier to show pictures of carnage with suggestions (subtle or otherwise).

---

23. *Children of Beslan*, HBO Documentary 2005.

10

FRAMING HOMELAND SECURITY

A. INTRODUCTION

Successful homeland security policy seeks to fulfill the state's obligation to protect the population while affecting the rights of individuals as little as reasonably possible. It is essential to recognize that not all assets can be equally protected. Prioritization of resources is mandatory.

Successful homeland security strategy requires cooperation among a broad range of government organizations. The cooperation required extends to multiple communities: law enforcement (local, state, and federal), intelligence gathering and analyzing, and the private sector (asset protection of business entities is a major issue). Cooperation must incorporate public-private information sharing in order to maximize both sector's ability to prevent and respond to acts of terrorism. Turf battles between bureaucracies and resource allocation disputes restrict the effective implementation of government policy.

This chapter will examine the efforts of the United States to implement a homeland security policy. While focusing on the United States, the following discussion can be analogized to any democratic state. In exploring the issue of homeland security, it will be necessary to determine what a state considers an effective policy and how it analyzes threats against the state. Once these questions are answered, we can begin to see how states strike a balance between the danger of collateral damage, reduced civil liberties, accountability to the legislative branch, fiscal responsibility, geopolitical concerns, and the rule of law.

B. EFFECTIVENESS

Determining what homeland security measures are effective requires defining criteria for measuring effectiveness. If a U.S. government agency can demonstrate empirically that a particular security measure will contribute to effective and legal counterterrorism, then it has merit. If the measure is yet another example of creating ad hoc counterterrorism policy not based on reliable and viable intelligence, then such a measure should be considered a "non-starter."

Lawmakers cannot wash their hands of a problem once they have established criteria to measure effectiveness. They must demand accountability from the executive. Without stringent accountability requirements, there is no guarantee that the executive will adhere to nor abide by the effectiveness criteria. This chapter also articulates accountability standards.

Effective counterterrorism causes the terrorist infrastructure to suffer serious damage, including damage to finances, resources, and personnel. Such measures potentially prevent a planned attack from going forth and/or postponing plans for future attacks while minimizing collateral damage, exercising fiscal responsibility, and preserving civil liberties.

1. Analyzing the Threat

The first step in creating an effective homeland security policy is analyzing the threat. To that end, the following questions must be answered:

1. **What is the threat the state faces?**
2. **Who is responsible for planning the threat?**
3. **Who is responsible for financing the threat?**
4. **Who is responsible for carrying out the threat?**
5. **When will the threat likely be carried out?**

Once these questions are answered, the threat can be placed on an imminent continuum with the understanding that one large threat may be comprised of smaller, more manageable threats. The imminent continuum has four major benchmarks: Imminent, Foreseeable, Long-range, and Uncertain.

Imminent threats are those that are to be shortly conducted; as an example a "hot" intelligence report suggests that a bomb will be detonated *tomorrow* at 9:11 A.M. at a domestic terminal at JFK airport.

Foreseeable threats are those that will be carried out *within a year* and are therefore more distant than an imminent threat. For example, a foreseeable threat includes valid intelligence that indicates that terrorists will shortly begin bringing explosives onto airplanes in liquid substances.

Long-range threats are specific threats that may reach fruition at an unknown time; for example, terrorist's training with no operational measure specifically planned would fit in this category.

Uncertain threats constitute those that invoke general fears of insecurity. As a result of train bombings in England and Spain travelers in the United States might potentially or conceivably feel insecure riding trains without bolstered security. This would be true regardless of whether there is valid intelligence indicating terrorists intend to start targeting trains in the United States.

Where a particular threat fits on the imminence continuum necessarily correlates to the balance that must be struck between national security and multiple competing interests. Figure 10.1 which depicts this

FIGURE 10.1 Balancing Factors

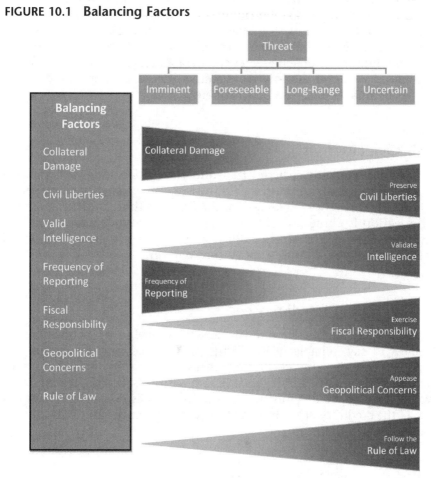

balance initially asks whether a threat is imminent, foreseeable, long-range, or uncertain. For example, more collateral damage is acceptable when a threat is imminent than when it is foreseeable, and the acceptable level of collateral damage continually decreases as the known imminence of a threat decreases. The preservation of civil liberties, however, is most significant when a threat is uncertain and becomes less significant as a threat becomes more imminent. At no point are any of these factors completely absent. They must always be considered and balanced in relation to the threat the nation faces.

2. Collateral Damage

The Geneva Conventions state that minimizing collateral damage is a requirement of international law and nations must limit collateral damage in times of war. Collateral damage requires minimizing the loss of civilian life in a military operation; proportionality requires that civilian losses be proportional to the military advantage. Ultimately, the public is willing to stomach greater collateral damage the more imminent a threat is. However, alternative effective measures that would lessen collateral damage must also be considered.

3. Civil Liberties

Liberal democratic societies that unilaterally decide on self-imposed restraints limit their responses to terrorism. However, balancing legitimate national security needs against the rights of those individuals living in the nation is a true test of a nation's adherence to democratic values. Any suspension of constitutionally guaranteed liberty must be weighed against legitimate national security considerations.

4. Verifying Intelligence

To be valid, intelligence must be reliable, viable, and corroborated. Needless to say, reliable, viable, and corroborated intelligence may be difficult to obtain. In all circumstances, reasonable effort should be made to obtain valid intelligence before action is taken. However, the level of imminence dictates the definition of "reasonable," with respect both to the credulity of the information and how much time is allotted for its corroboration.

5. Frequency of Reporting

This factor encompasses the forthcoming accountability discussion. While Congress has mandated annual reports on terrorist threats, these reports are too infrequent with respect to imminent and foreseeable threats and possibly inapplicable to uncertain threats. Counterterrorism measures taken to address imminent threats should be reported to Congress after the threat has passed. Only in this manner can Congress have meaningful review of executive actions.

Foreseeable threats should be reported to Congress when the threat is identified. This would enable Congress to coordinate efforts, and better understand how various agencies detect and counter various threats.

Many uncertain threats will not fall within the scope of the federal government. For example, California requires the State Department of Education to electronically distribute disaster preparedness materials and lesson plans to school districts. Threats that do implicate the federal government, however, may appropriately be addressed when agencies address long-range threats. State legislatures should implement reporting procedures for uncertain threats that exist on a state level.

6. Fiscal Responsibility

Financial costs necessarily limit the quantity of counterterrorism measures a nation may conduct. With limited resources, government must pick and choose which measures will most effectively counter short- and long-term threats. Although the need for fiscal responsibility lessens as a threat becomes more imminent, planning for potential attacks will allow careful use of financial resources even in the face of imminent threats. This would, thereby, free resources for countering long-range and uncertain threats. Thus, financial responsibility contributes to an overarching security strategy.

7. Geopolitical Concerns

Counterterrorism necessarily raises international concerns because the threat does not reside exclusively within a nation's borders. The court of international opinion should be considered when selecting a particular counterterrorism measure. Wrong choices cause the United States to lose global influence and/or minimize the ability to persuade vulnerable "swayables" from becoming terrorists. Homeland security measures must give weight to geopolitical considerations, though with an imminent threat geopolitical concerns may necessarily take a back seat.

8. Rule of Law

In order to best adhere to the rule of law, counterterrorism measures should be drafted in advance of such an actual threat. Such measures should dictate which laws may be relaxed and to what extent when facing an imminent threat. To wait until a threat is present denies government the opportunity to make careful and conscious choices that will provide security to the public while balancing their rights.

C. HOMELAND SECURITY

The U.S. federal government currently defines homeland security as "a concerted national effort to prevent terrorist attacks within the United States, reduce America's vulnerability to terrorism, and minimize the damage and recover from attacks that do occur." The Department of Defense clarifies that "external" threats may arise internally and the term "external" does not limit where or how attacks could be executed. The following is an excerpt from the Bush Administration's National Strategy for Homeland Security:

> The United States, through a concerted national effort that galvanizes the strengths and capabilities of Federal, State, local, and Tribal governments; the private and non-profit sectors; and regions, communities, and individual citizens—along with our partners in the international community—will work to achieve a secure Homeland that sustains our way of life as a free, prosperous, and welcoming America. In order to realize this vision, the United States will use all instruments of national power and influence—diplomatic, information, military, economic, financial, intelligence, and law enforcement—to achieve our goals to prevent and disrupt terrorist attacks; protect the American people, critical infrastructure, and key resources; and respond to and recover from incidents that do occur. We also will continue to create, strengthen, and transform the principles, systems, structures, and institutions we need to secure our Nation over the long term. This is our strategy for homeland security.[1]

The current definition of homeland security is unworkable for two major reasons: it does not sufficiently emphasize the requirement to protect individual rights with respect to the rights of the state, and it does not

---

1. Available at http://www.globalsecurity.org/security/library/report/2007/nshs-200710.htm/.

provide a realistic framework regarding the government's ability to respond to threats.

Priorities must be established according to threat analysis and fiscal limits that the public will support. In examining government policy in the aftermath of 9/11, the lack of a concentrated and realistic focus is dramatically apparent. Seeking to protect against all threats at all times creates an overreaching policy that inevitably results in violations of civil rights and liberties. A more systematic approach that critically examines prioritization, threat assessment, and risk assessment in the context of cost-benefit analysis suggests a more realistic and effective definition of homeland security:

> A group of preventative measures undertaken by a state in an attempt to reduce the probability that a terrorist attack will occur. This strategy will be fluid, constantly reassessing the balance between rights of the individual and rights of the state. A realistic strategy must prioritize threats according to their probability and imminence.

1. Differentiating Homeland Security from Other Terms

An attempt to further refine the definition of homeland security requires distinguishing it from a similar term in the counterterrorism lexicon, specifically "homeland defense" and "counterterrorism."

Homeland defense, as defined by the Department of Defense in its *Strategy for Homeland Defense and Civil Support*, is "the protection of U.S. sovereignty, territory, domestic population, and critical defense infrastructure against external threats and aggression, or other threats as described by the President." The Department of Defense clarifies that "external" threats may arise internally, and the term "external" does not limit "where or how attacks could be executed."

Counterterrorism: The actions of a state, proactive or reactive, intended to kill or injure terrorists and/or to cause serious significant damage to the terrorist's infrastructure.

The difference between homeland defense and homeland security might correspond roughly to the difference between "reaction" versus "prevention." As Professor Wayne McCormack points out in *Legal Responses to Terrorism*, while the political world and the media sometimes lump all responses to terrorism together under the label "counterterrorism," that term "is more appropriately used for prosecutorial and military-type responses while preventative measures are more aptly characterized as 'anti-terrorism.'"[2] Homeland security, as defined by the federal government, meshes better with the concept of antiterrorism, or prevention.

Homeland security, distinct from national defense, was established in Executive Order 13228, which created the Office of Homeland Security within the Executive Office of the President. This order identifies key homeland security functions: "to detect, prepare for, prevent, protect against, respond to, and recover from terrorist attacks within the United States."

2. Structuring Homeland Security

Numerous state, federal, and municipal agencies work together to ensure public safety in the United States. These include law enforcement, first responders, the military, and public health officials who coordinate activities with the relevant local community's infrastructure.

The U.S. must be protected against both terrorism (international and domestic) and catastrophic events, including natural disasters and man-made accidents. Scholars have suggested three priorities with respect to homeland security: border security, critical infrastructure protection, and intelligence analysis.[3]

a. Prevent and Disrupt Terrorist Attacks

The Bush Administration has articulated the absolute importance of denying terrorists access to weapons of mass destruction (WMDs) by detecting, disrupting, and interdicting the movement of WMD-related materials. The administration seeks to coordinate the efforts of all levels of government, the private sector, foreign allies, and international and domestic institutions in order to:

- Determine terrorists' intentions, capabilities, and plans to develop or acquire WMD;
- Deny terrorists access to the material, expertise, and other enabling capabilities required to develop WMD;
- Deter terrorists from employing WMD;
- Detect and disrupt terrorists' attempted movement of WMD-related materials, weapons, and personnel;

---

2. WAYNE McCORMACK, LEGAL RESPONSES TO TERRORISM (2005).

3. Paul Light & James Lindsay, Council on Foreign Relations, Views of Homeland Security (2002), http://www.cfr.org/publication/6395/views_of_homeland_security.html.

- Prevent and respond to a WMD-related terrorist attack; and
- Define the nature and source of a terrorist-employed WMD device.

b. Border Control and Immigration

Control and management of the nation's borders and immigration into the nation are critical in achieving effective homeland security. According to the Bush Administration, the following measures are critical:

- Improve ability to detain and remove criminal and fugitive aliens and visa violators
- Hire, train, and deploy additional Border Patrol agents, Customs and Border Protection officers, and Immigration and Customs Enforcement officers
- Build on the substantial improvements to the infrastructure and technology deployed at our borders
- Expand detention bed space for aliens subject to detention and removal
- Enhance interior enforcement efforts, including worksite enforcement programs.

In addition, the Bush Administration emphasizes that employers must verify the work eligibility of all employees. This is intended to prevent illegal immigrants from obtaining jobs through fraud or the use of stolen identification, including Social Security numbers. In order to accomplish this, the Administration suggests that the nation:

- Expand the use of an electronic employment eligibility verification system that is timely, accurate, and easy for employers to use;
- Crack down on employers who knowingly hire illegal immigrants by applying criminal penalties to those who circumvent the law; and
- Step up efforts to verify the status of non-immigrants studying in the United States through the Student and Exchange Visitor Information System (SEVIS) and have appropriate follow-up where there may be violations.

c. Critical Infrastructure

Critical infrastructure is defined as the "systems and assets, whether physical or virtual, so vital to the United States that the incapacity or destruction of such systems and assets would have a debilitating impact on security, national economic security, or any combination of those matters."[4] The Office of Homeland Security has identified 17 sectors of critical infrastructure and key resources:

1. Agriculture and Food
2. Banking and Finance
3. Chemical
4. Commercial Facilities
5. Commercial Nuclear Reactors, Materials, and Waste
6. Dams
7. Defense Industrial Base
8. Drinking Water and Water Treatment Systems
9. Emergency Services
10. Energy
11. Government Facilities
12. Information Technology
13. National Monuments and Icons
14. Postal and Shipping
15. Public Health and Health Care
16. Telecommunications
17. Transportation Systems

---

4. Symposium, *Homeland Security, Law, and Policy Through the Lens of Critical Infrastructure and Key Asset Protection*, 47 Jurimetrics J. 259, 260 (2007).

D. GLOBAL PERSPECTIVES ON HOMELAND SECURITY

In the aftermath of 9/11, the United States was forced to decide for the first time how it would structure a broad-scale, permanent antiterrorism infrastructure. It is beneficial to compare the U.S.'s approach with how other nations respond to terrorism and develop and implement counter-terrorism efforts. To that end, briefly highlighted below are the efforts of Israel and the United Kingdom. The approaches of both nations—in response to the "daily grind of terrorism" (unlike 9/11)—is particularly noteworthy because their respective policies are measured, not overbroad, and reflect sensitivity to the need to prioritize and develop sophisticated risk and threat assessment mechanisms.

Rather than adopting an overreaching policy, with all of its attendant weaknesses and vulnerabilities, both Israel and the United Kingdom have adopted and implemented a policy which reflects an understanding that not all national infrastructures can be equally protected. The requirement to systemically prioritize is critical.

1. Israel

Israel's homeland security efforts fall under the Ministry of Public Security. Described broadly, the duties of this ministry are:

> To make policy and monitor its implementation, to take necessary decisions and see them carried out, to allocate resources to the executive arms and monitor their use, to consider and respond to the demands, proposals and plans put to the Ministry by its field agencies, to receive and process complaints from within the law enforcement system and the general public and draw lessons, to promote new legislation required by the police and prison services, and to represent the interests of the Ministry in dealings with other ministries and public private agencies.[5]

The Israel National Police (INP), one of the two executive agencies under the Ministry of Public Security, is most directly responsible for what is basically analogous to U.S. homeland security. The two major units of the INP are the Investigations Department and the Operations and Patrol Department. The Investigations Department heads both the Criminal Identification Division and the Intelligence Division. The Operations and Patrol Department is responsible for all of the daily activities of the INP, including "maintenance of civil order, ... crime prevention, [and]

---

5. Israel Ministry of Foreign Affairs, *Ministry of Public Security* (2003), *available at* http://www.mfa.gov.il/MFA/MFAArchive/2000_2009/2003/3/Ministry%20of%20Public%20Security.

anti-terrorist activities." The Bomb Disposal Division "operates in the realm of both criminal and terrorist sabotage activities" and responds to approximately 80,000 calls annually.

The Israeli Civil Guard was created in direct response to a series of terrorist attacks in 1974. It is a volunteer force comprising a network of neighborhood command centers, armed mobile and foot patrols, and rapid emergency response teams. The volunteer force numbers about 45,000, and must participate in regular police training and target practice.

What is important to note is that Israel's homeland security measures are conducted in an integrative manner, enabling more effective cooperation between relevant government (national and local) agencies. While turf battles and disagreement regarding jurisdictional authority are inevitable, the Israeli model enables policy and decision makers to more effectively determine prioritization, threat assessment, and risk assessment precisely because it is predicated on an integrative approach.

2. United Kingdom

The United Kingdom's approach, similar to Israel's, has been formulated over decades of responding to terrorist threats and other security challenges. The British government's counterterrorism strategy (known as CONTEST) focuses on the "4 Ps" — prevent, pursue, protect, and prepare.

The UK approach to homeland security emphasizes measures that integrate counterterrorism and disaster preparedness plans into currently existing emergency management and response programs. This dual-use approach implements the existing skills and training of various departments, agencies, and first responders to the overall strategy of preventing terrorist attacks. That being said, one of the central concerns (similar to the United States) of the British intergovernmental approach to homeland security is the poor coordination between departments with blurred lines of authority.

E. ACCOUNTABILITY

The 9/11 Commission's Report emphasizes in detail the need for standards of accountability in developing and implementing counterterrorism measures. The 9/11 Commission correctly stated that "effective public policies … need concrete objectives."[6] That is, in

---

6. National Commission on Terrorist Attacks Upon the United States, The 9/11 Commission Report Executive Summary 364 (2004).

the struggle against terrorism, "agencies need to be able to measure success:"[7]

> These measurements do not need to be quantitative: government cannot measure success in the ways that private firms can. But the targets should be specific enough so that reasonable observers—in the White House, the Congress, the media, or the general public—can judge whether or not the objectives have been attained.
>
> Vague goals match an amorphous picture of the enemy. Al Qaeda and its affiliates are popularly described as being all over the world, adaptable, resilient, needing little higher-level organization, and capable of anything. The American people are thus given the picture of an omnipotent, unslayable hydra of destruction. This image lowers expectations for government effectiveness.
>
> ...
>
> We do not believe it is possible to defeat all terrorist attacks against Americans, every time and everywhere.... But the American people are entitled to expect their government to do its very best. They should expect that officials will have realistic objectives, clear guidance, and effective organization. They are entitled to see some standards for performance so they can judge, with the help of their elected representatives, whether the objectives are being met.[8]

The 9/11 Commission Report appropriately calls for objective standards of accountability through which the effectiveness of counterterrorism measures can be measured. As discussed in Chapter 6, checks and balances are critical to creating effective counterterrorism policy. They are similarly essential to homeland security.

F. CONCLUSION

Defining terms is essential to this discussion; without articulating effectiveness and accountability in the context of homeland security it is all but impossible to develop and implement policies. Without adequate definitions establishing subject matter responsibility for local, state, and federal agencies, cooperation among these entities (not to mention with the private sector) will be all but impossible. Policy and decision makers must know how to "operationalize" the relevant aspects discussed in this chapter. Otherwise, homeland security—similar to counterterrorism—will be nothing more than a very expensive groping in the dark.

---

7. National Commission on Terrorist Attacks Upon the United States, The 9/11 Commission Report Executive Summary 364 (2004).

8. National Commission on Terrorist Attacks Upon the United States, The 9/11 Commission Report Executive Summary 364-365 (2004).

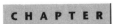

GOING FORWARD

A. INTRODUCTION

Nineteen years of involvement in operational counterterrorism have taught me many lessons in this most complex of fields. There are constantly new developments in counterterrorism, both domestically and internationally. Effective counterterrorism requires new thinking and creativity. At the same time, however, there are certain lessons that will always be a constant—and if these lessons are not learned, all the creativity in the world will not result in effective counterterrorism strategy.

History has repeatedly shown that terrorism cannot be defeated by overwhelming force. A state seeking to manage terrorism must understand that limits are critical to lawful and effective counterterrorism. The state must clearly articulate its goals. Exercising power without articulated benchmarks for success will be an exercise in futility and all but guarantees violations of civil rights. Furthermore, unrestrained use of force will significantly contribute to blowback, continuing a never-ending cycle of violence. Finally, a state must combine a forceful counterterrorism policy with other long-term strategies—empowering moderate groups, promoting education and economic development. If these lessons are forgotten, democratic societies will succeed at nothing but causing themselves enormous damage in the fight against terrorism.

Defining effectiveness is predicated on risk- and threat-assessment. This requires sophisticated intelligence gathering and analysis. Otherwise, operational counterterrorism is best described as "groping in the dark" with significant human rights violations all but guaranteed. Intelligence is the heart and soul of operational counterterrorism. It is painstaking, requiring extraordinary patience and the ability to connect unseen dots.

Commanders are invariably frustrated by the slowness of the intelligence analysis process—the desire to act must be tempered by care and caution. Collateral damage is the inevitable result of haste. The long-term consequences of collateral damage in the sophisticated media age go far beyond a particular decision made by one commander. That is why effectiveness must be defined. Decision makers who adopt a "larger picture" approach to operational counterterrorism will be driven by the following considerations:

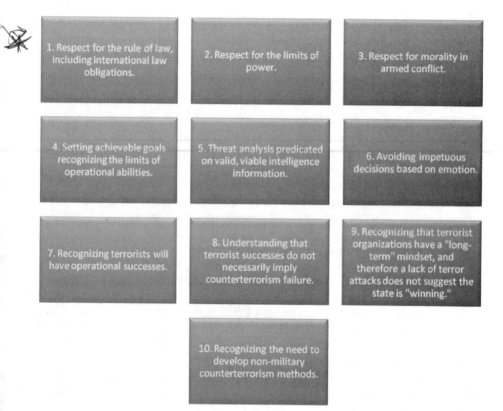

1. Respect for the rule of law, including international law obligations.

2. Respect for the limits of power.

3. Respect for morality in armed conflict.

4. Setting achievable goals recognizing the limits of operational abilities.

5. Threat analysis predicated on valid, viable intelligence information.

6. Avoiding impetuous decisions based on emotion.

7. Recognizing terrorists will have operational successes.

8. Understanding that terrorist successes do not necessarily imply counterterrorism failure.

9. Recognizing that terrorist organizations have a "long-term" mindset, and therefore a lack of terror attacks does not suggest the state is "winning."

10. Recognizing the need to develop non-military counterterrorism methods.

B. PICKING YOUR BATTLES

Commanders and decision makers must understand that the threat of terror attacks is constant. Nevertheless, in the context of lawful counterterrorism, the public must understand that limits on power are an absolute requirement. In addition, decision makers must recognize that not every threat is valid and viable.

During the course of my career I was repeatedly requested to provide legal advice regarding specific intelligence-based threats. The legal advice was both person-specific (detention, administrative sanction, targeted killing) and group- or community-specific (curfew). The obligation was to balance powerful competing interests under significant pressure. Luxury of time was not an option. That is precisely why the ten-point check list is critical to decision and policy makers. The reality of competing pressures highlights the need to develop—in advance—workable checklists that seek to minimize preventable and regrettable mistakes.

While commanders and legal advisors may disagree regarding particular items on a checklist, all those involved must agree on the fundamental principle that the state is subservient to the rule of law.

C. HOW WILL A DECISION BE VIEWED BY THE COMMUNITY?

While particular terrorist attacks are especially venomous, the instinctual response must be tempered. Lashing out only serves the terrorist organizations long-term goals. Victimology combined with alienation and humiliation is critical to a terrorist organization playing to multiple audiences—existing membership and potential recruits.

The reality of the "all seeing camera" is skillfully used by terrorist leaders, many of them particularly adroit at manipulating events to their advantage. The underdog (victimology) is an easier media sell than a state spokesman explaining why a particular counterterrorism operation (even if justified) killed a number of innocent individuals.

Terrorist organizations skillfully manipulate symbols to their advantage. When the French and Turkish governments banned Islamic women from wearing scarfs to school (high school and medical school), religious and cultural leaders were able to galvanize supporters by claiming that the state was violating tenets of the faith. Perhaps the state's decision was correct; perhaps not. What is clear is that the decision "benefits" fundamentalists in the context of justifying a response (whether the response is immediate or delayed is irrelevant). This is particularly the case when terrorists are religiously motivated—the concept of duty and obligation to God is a powerful motivator for extremists.

D. IS INTELLIGENCE SOLID?

Operational counterterrorism decision-making is intelligence-dependent. Pragmatically, this requires an objective analysis of the received intelligence in order to corroborate its veracity. To that end, information must meet a recommended four-part test:

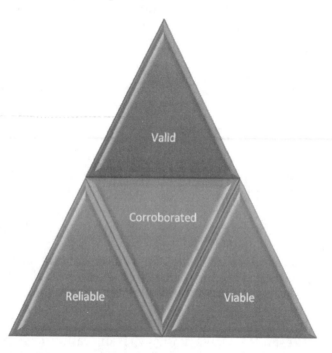

Decision-making based on (1) respect for the rule of law in conjunction with (2) the four-part intelligence test and the (3) ten-point checklist of effectiveness criteria would contribute to more sophisticated operational counterterrorism.

While difficult to implement, the proposed three-part model would enable decision makers to address and implement many of the issues discussed in this book. That model suggests an approach significantly different from existing models because the emphasis is on analyzing options, decisions, and their ramifications.

E. A NEW VISION OF SELF-DEFENSE

Understanding counterterrorism—this book's aim—is incomplete without addressing self-defense. When and under what circumstances may a nation-state attack the non-state actor? Determining when the intelligence is actionable is the essence of operational decision-making.

When a nation-state may use self-defense as a justification for action has been articulated in three international law standards (*Caroline* doctrine,[1] Article 51,[2] and UN Resolutions 1368,[3] 1373[4]). In general, nations adhere to these standards in an effort to meet the four international law principles (collateral damage, proportionality, military assistance, and alternatives) that govern the laws of war.[5] However, unlike days when armies lined up on their borders, announcing their impending invasion, non-state actors are largely amorphous and invisible until the moment of attack.

In an effort to balance between the need to enable the state to more effectively protect its citizens (thereby institutionalizing preventive

---

1. In 1837, U.S. Secretary of State Daniel Webster articulated a definition of self-defense that eventually evolved into customary international law. Webster's definition followed what has come to be known as the *Caroline* incident. The *Caroline* was a U.S. steamboat attempting to transport supplies to Canadian insurgents. A British force interrupted the *Caroline*'s voyage, shot at it, set it on fire and let it wash over Niagara Falls. Webster said that Britain's act did not qualify as self-defense because self-defense is only justified "if the necessity of that self-defense is instant, overwhelming, and leaving no choice of means, and no moment for deliberation." According to Webster, Britain could have dealt with the *Caroline* in a more diplomatic manner. He limited the right to self-defense to situations where there is a real threat, the response is essential and proportional, and all peaceful means of resolving the dispute have been exhausted. His idea is now known as the *Caroline* doctrine, and was considered customary international law until a competing definition arose in Article 51 of the UN Charter. Letter from Daniel Webster, U.S. Sec'y of State, to Lord Ashburton, British Special Minister (July 27, 1842), *available at* http://www.yale.edu/lawweb/avalon/diplomacy/britain/br-1842d.htm.

2. U.N. CHARTER, art. 51, states that "Nothing in the present Charter shall impair the inherent right of individual or collective self-defence if an armed attack occurs against a Member of the United Nations, until the Security Council has taken measures necessary to maintain international peace and security. Measures taken by Members in the exercise of this right of self-defence shall be immediately reported to the Security Council and shall not in any way affect the authority and responsibility of the Security Council under the present Charter to take at any time such action as it deems necessary in order to maintain or restore international peace and security."

3. S.C. Res. 1368, U.N. Doc. S/Res/1368 (Sept. 12, 2001). The UN Security Council adopted a resolution condemning the 9/11 terrorist attacks and calls upon "all States to work together urgently to bring to justice the perpetrators, organizers and sponsors of these terrorist attacks and *stresses* that those responsible for aiding, supporting or harbouring the perpetrators, organizers and sponsors of these acts will be held accountable."

4. S.C. Res. 1373, U.N. SCOR, 57th Sess., 4385th mtg., U.N. Doc. S/RES/1373 (2001). The U.N. Security Council issued a statement calling on states to prevent and suppress the financing of terrorist acts, and "refrain from providing any form of support, active or passive, to entities or persons involved in terrorist acts."

5. See Chapter 4 for further discussion.

self-defense) and the need to protect innocent civilians living among terrorists (thereby minimizing collateral damage), I suggest that post-9/11 self-defense be re-articulated.

Self-defense justifies state action *earlier* than international norms currently dictate *provided* that the available intelligence meets the four-part test discussed in this book: reliability, validity, viability, and corroboration.[6] At a minimum, in order to justify operational decisions, I suggest intelligence information meet an "admissible to a court of law" standard. The table below illustrates the basis of the strict scrutiny model.

FUNDAMENTAL RIGHT	THE STATE HAS A FUNDAMENTAL RIGHT TO SELF-DEFENSE
State's Primary Responsibility	The State's primary responsibility is to protect the safety and welfare of its citizens.
Operational Counterterrorism	Operational counterterrorism must be predicated on the rule of law, morality in armed conflict, and effective policy.
Intelligence Admissible to a Court of Law	Actionable intelligence must meet an "admissibility to a court of law" test.

Let us examine and then apply each leg to operational reality. The question is when and under what circumstances may the state act in accordance with lawful self-defense. The guiding premise is that states can protect themselves *earlier* in time based on intelligence information provided it meets the admissibility test. The strict scrutiny test seeks to establish objective criteria prior to operational action. Remember that the Barak theory (self-imposed restraints) espouses both *protected* categories — citizens and innocent civilians — must be equally protected. While that theory has come under fire for limiting operational counterterrorism, in the long run it creates a more effective, person-specific strategy that eliminates unwanted byproducts of more shortsighted operations.

Strict scrutiny suggests acting earlier against an *unprotected* category of legitimate targets. The application of the scrutiny — which leads to more effective and *earlier* targeting of legitimate targets — suggests that greater protection will be offered to both *protected* classes.

---

6. See Chapter 5 for further discussion.

Application of the strict scrutiny test still allows the state to meet the four international law principles that are the heart and soul of the laws of war. The four principles are intended to govern the relationship between the state and protected civilians in the context of armed conflict. Much as the Constitution articulates the rights of the people, these international law principles lay the foundation for the relationship between nation-states and individuals otherwise unprotected.

In laying the foundation for this relationship, these four principles represent the limits of power. That is, the principles exercise control on how far — and when — the state can protect itself. To that end, the strict scrutiny test respects that limitation *while* facilitating more elastic yet more precise state action. Rather than violating those four principles, application of the strict scrutiny test would ensure greater respect of international law.

Perhaps the Clinton bombing of the Sudanese pharmaceutical factory best exemplifies the merits of the strict scrutiny test.[7] By not subjecting the available intelligence to principles governing admissibility of evidence in a courtroom, a pharmaceutical company rather than chemical making plant was targeted. Some may argue that operational errors are inevitable; I would suggest that while combat inherently involves (if not invites) mistakes and tragedy, the state is obligated to minimize such occurrences.

F. MAKING A DECISION

From here we reach the critical question — how do decision makers *know* that the available intelligence indeed justifies state action? What are the standards that are to be used? Counterterrorism must be predicated on objective standards. What is the process that will directly lead to more measured, and therefore more effective, operational decisions?

That world is comprised of sources (sometimes with their own agenda), case officers, terrorists, decision makers' legal advisors, and operators (those who operationally engage the terrorist). It is a complicated community. Hesitation to pull the trigger may simultaneously spare the life of a terrorist while directly contributing to the death of an

---

7. In 1998, the United States destroyed a factory in Khartoum, Sudan in retaliation for attacks on U.S. embassies in several African countries. The U.S. argued that the factory had ties to al-Qaeda and was being used for processing deadly nerve agents. Officials later acknowledged that the evidence that prompted President Clinton to order to attack was not solid, as the factory was used to manufacture pharmaceuticals.

innocent civilian; wrong decisions may result in innocent deaths. For example, following the assassination of Israeli athletes in the 1972 Munich Olympics, Israeli operatives killed Ahmed Bouchiki, an innocent Moroccan waiter who was mistaken for Ali Hassan Salameh, the commander of Yasser Arafat's personal security squad. Six operatives were arrested for Bouchiki's murder in 1973.

Another example illustrates the issue: In requesting permission to shoot to kill, a commander was presented the following facts. According to the intelligence community, an individual dressed in a certain manner and carrying a particular bag would — if not killed — present a grave threat to national security. The operational window of opportunity available to the commander was limited to a few minutes. Troops had been strategically placed in position. The individual in question walked like and carried a bag similar to the presented intelligence. But was he the same person?

That was the dilemma I faced with when called by the commander. In preparation for such a request, I had developed a checklist of questions for those seeking my authorization for such decisions. Those questions included:

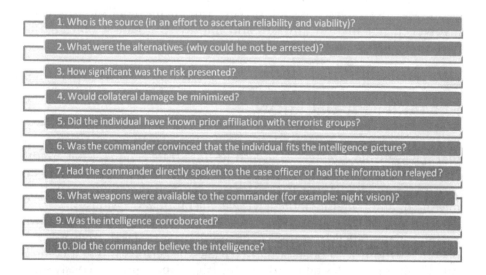

1. Who is the source (in an effort to ascertain reliability and viability)?

2. What were the alternatives (why could he not be arrested)?

3. How significant was the risk presented?

4. Would collateral damage be minimized?

5. Did the individual have known prior affiliation with terrorist groups?

6. Was the commander convinced that the individual fits the intelligence picture?

7. Had the commander directly spoken to the case officer or had the information relayed?

8. What weapons were available to the commander (for example: night vision)?

9. Was the intelligence corroborated?

10. Did the commander believe the intelligence?

These questions were predicated on the state's fundamental right to self-defense and therefore ensure the legality of operational counterterrorism. But, just as importantly, they reflected a refusal to "say yes" (killing the individual) solely based on what was reported to the commander regarding the content of a conversation between the source and a case officer. The risks (killing an innocent individual) are too great to answer in the affirmative based on limited facts or information. In correlating this dilemma to the criminal law process, the questions are similar:

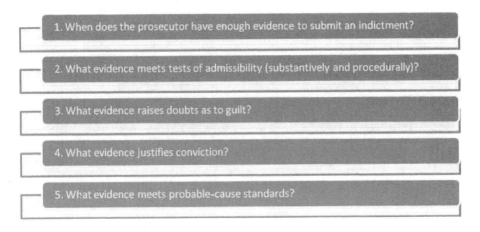

1. When does the prosecutor have enough evidence to submit an indictment?

2. What evidence meets tests of admissibility (substantively and procedurally)?

3. What evidence raises doubts as to guilt?

4. What evidence justifies conviction?

5. What evidence meets probable-cause standards?

G. CONCLUSION

While the criminal law process is predicated on separation of powers (the prosecutor represents the executive branch, the judge represents the judiciary, and the defense attorney represents the accused), operational counterterrorism is *on its face* devoid of legislative oversight or judicial review. The advantage of process-predicated input *prior* to an executive decision is worthy of discussion even in operational counterterrorism. The stakes are too high.

The process-driven approach is the intellectual backbone of the strict scrutiny test. The strict scrutiny test suggests that while the state can act earlier than is presently the norm, the intelligence justifying the proposed action must be submitted to a court that would ascertain the information's admissibility. The discussion before the court would necessarily be conducted *ex parte*. However, the process of preparing and submitting available intelligence to a court would significantly contribute to minimizing operational error that otherwise would occur. Rather than requiring the executive to submit intelligence to an independent judiciary for authorization of an operational decision, a commission of experts might be the more appropriate body.

The critical question is how to prevent executive excess within the context of limiting state power while ensuring that citizens are protected. That is the essence of the self-defense debate and also the key to understanding effective counterterrorism.

INDEX

Abbas, Mahmoud, 49
Abu Ghraib, 106-107, 114. *See also* Interrogation of terrorism suspects
Abu Sayyaf, 48
Addington, David, 94
Administrative detention. *See* Detention
Airport security, 21
Akhmedova, Khapta, 37
Al Qaeda. *See also* September 11, 2001 attacks on United States
  in Afghanistan, 56
  differences between Hamas and franchises, 58
  franchises, 54-59
  global terrorists vs. geographic-specific, 48
  in Iraq, 63
  manifesto, 34
  targets, 54-55
Amir, Yigal, 15
Amnesty International
  report on Guantanamo Bay, 113
Arafat, Yasser, 34, 148
Armstrong, Jack, 146
Army Field Manual
  on torture, 105

Ashcroft, John, 95
Assassination
  at Munich Olympics, 172
  of political leaders, 18
  planned for President Bush, 135
Authorization for Use of Military Force (AUMF), 91-92, 97. *See also* September 11, 2001 attacks on United States
Ayalon, Chief-of-Staff Moshe (Bugi), 143

Baader-Meinhof, 32
Bali bombing, 54, 55, 127
Barak, Aharon
  on judicial activism in armed conflict, 93-94
  on self-imposed restraints, 65-66, 170
Bennett, W.L., 141
Berg, Nicholas, 146
Beslan schoolhouse attack. *See also* Chechens; Media
  international opinion, 149
Bigley, Kenneth, 146
bin Laden, Osama. *See also* Al Qaeda
  attacks responsible for, 55-56

fighting Soviets in Afghanistan, 60

and franchise terror organizations, 56-58

and Russian accusation of "double standard," 11

Bombings, 18-21, 31, 36, 66, 127, 134, 140, 148. *See also* specific location of bombings

suicide, 41-44, 48

Bush Administration. *See also* United States

Afghanistan attacks post-9/11, 127

border control, 159

on detention, 73

FISA and, 97

and homeland security, 156-157

Iraq War and, 60

WMDs and, 158

and lack of congressional oversight, 91-92, 96-97

on torture, 108-109

Bush Doctrine, 126-127, 129, 135

Bybee-Yoo memo, 107

Cali, Dennis D., 141

Caroline incident and doctrine, 124, 131, 169

CAT (Convention Against Torture), 95, 106, 115

Chechens, 11, 15, 40, 48

Beslan schoolhouse attack, 149

Checks and balances

congressional oversight, need for, 94-96

executive self-restraint, 99

judiciary, 98

public, 98

media, 99

The Judge Advocate Generals (TJAGs), 96

Cheney, Vice President Dick, 94, 114

CIA role in torture of detainees, 105-106, 113

Clinton, President,

bombing of Iraqi Military Intelligence headquarters, 133, 135

bombing of Sudanese pharmaceutical factory, 171

Cohen-Almagor, Raphael, 143-144

Cole, USS, 55, 62, 141

Coll, Steve, 60

Collateral damage, 14, 22, 28, 65-70, 81, 151-152, 154, 165. *See also* Innocent civilians

Combatants. *See also* Detention; Enemy combatants

distinguishing between non-combatants, 86

status review for U.S. detainees, 113

Combs, Cindy, 35

Confessions. *See* Interrogation of terrorists

Counterterrorism

defined, 26

developing a strategy, 26

effectiveness, 152-156

and geopolitics, 47-60

self-defense. *See* Self-defense

targeted killing, 81-87

three models of, 27

Crenshaw, Martha, 39

Criminal law paradigm

classification of terrorist-defendants, 71-72

intelligence gathering and, 173

similarities to counterterrorim policies regarding "open fire" orders, 83-85

Dershowitz, Alan, 107

Detention

detention centers, 111

Guantanamo Bay. *See also* Guantanamo Bay detainees

indefinite detentions, 95

trials of detainees, 95

and hybrid paradigm, 72-73

Israel

active judical review, 103

limits of, 113-114
rights of detainees, 72
United States. *See also* Enemy
    combatants
    combatant status review
        tribunals, 113
    interrogation methods. *See*
        Interrogation of terrorism
        suspects
    military commissions. *See*
        Military commissions (U.S.)
    rights of accused, 100

Ecoterrorism
    Animal Liberation Front, 15
    Earth Liberation Front, 15
Elliot, Deni, 141
Embassy bombings in Kenya and
    Tanzania, 55
Enemy combatants, 71
    and *Boumediene v. Bush*, 98
England, Lynndie, 114
European Court of Human Rights,
    108

Fatwa, 56, 62
Federal Bureau of Investigation
    (FBI), 18, 19, 33
    definition of cyberterrorism,
        18
    definition of terrorism, 11
Foreign Intelligence Surveillance
    Act (FISA), 97
Frederick, Army Reserve Staff Sgt.
    Chip, 106
Friedman, Thomas, 146
Fujimoto, Shun, 116

Gaza Strip. *See* Israel
General Security Service (GSS),
    30
Geneva Conventions, 95, 107,
    154
Ghanayem, Abd al-Hadi, 17

Global Islamic terrorism
    existence of, 47-49
    Hamas as case study, 49-53
Gonzales, Attorney General, 107
Guantanamo Bay detainees
    Boumediene v. Bush, 98
    establishment of detention camp
        at, 95
    failures due to lack of oversight,
        95, 113
    interrogation of. *See* Interrogation
        of terrorism suspects
    pictures from, 113

Habeas corpus, writs of, 98
Hamas, 15, 48, 49-54, 61, 62, 63,
    123. *See also* Global Islamic
    terrorism
    compared to al Qaeda, 54, 58
    compared to al Qaeda franchises,
        58
    compared to PLO, 53
    defined, 49
    dependence on Islamic charities,
        125
    Palestinian Authority elections,
        49
    suicide bombings (Fall 2000),
        147
    support for, 51-52
    television, 38
Harakat ul-Mujahedeen, 49
Hensley, Jack, 146
Hezbollah, 48, 51, 54,
    125-128
    acting on behalf of Iran, 124
    Syria as conduit for, 134
Hoffman, Bruce, 8
Homeland security, 151-163
    effectiveness, 151-156
    fiscal responsibility, 155
    differentiated from homeland
        defense and
        counterterrorism, 157
    geopolitical concerns, 155
    structure, 158-160

Hostage situation in Iran (1979),
    143-144
Human Rights Watch
    on China, 9-10
    on counterterrorism, 28
Human shields, 67, 69
Huntington, Samuel, 49
Hussain, Hasib, 57
Hussein, Saddam, 62
    link to 9/11, 60

Ideology. *See* Terrorism
Improvised Explosive Devices (IED)
    attacks, 60-61
India
    antiterrorism ordinance, 10
Individual rights vs. national
    security, 93
    narrowing due to terrorism, 109
    prioritizing between, 157
Innocent civilians
    collateral damage, 65-70
    distinguishing from legitimate
        targets, 8
    media coverage of innocent
        civilian attacks, 147
    and open fire orders, 83
    protection of, 85-87
    risks of killing, 61
    targeting of, 14, 20
Intelligence gathering, 26, 105, 114
    homeland security, 151
Intelligence information
    reliability of, 80, 154
    types of
        human intelligence
            (HUMINT), 80
        open (newspapers, Internet), 81
        signal intelligence (SIGINT), 81
International law. *See also specific
    conventions*
    collateral damage minimization
        requirement, 69-70
    and limits of power, 65-70
    obligations under, 66, 69
    relationship between states, 123

self-defense principles. *See* Self-
    defense
    and terrorist suspects, 70-72
    U.S. policy and, 71
Internment camps for Japanese-
    Americans, 98
Interrogation of terrorism suspects,
    105-121
    Abu Ghraib
        effects of, 113
        permissible techniques, 107-
            108
    coercive interrogation
        distinguished from torture,
            118-119
    legal-judicial infrastructure, 121
    and the public, 120
Intifada, 87, 116, 143
Intimidation
    definition, 13
Iran, 40, 54, 63, 134
    and Hezbolla, 124-126, 128, 129
    hostage taking (1979), 143-144
Iraq, 40, 52
    al Qaeda in, 63
    and global jihadism, 62
    IED attacks in, 60-61
    Spanish withdrawal from, 58, 59
    U.S. war on, 60-63
Irish Republican Army (IRA), 34,
    123, 125
    and Sinn Fein, 41
Islamic Jihad, 36, 48
Israel
    and Hamas, 49, 62
    and Hezbollah, 127-128
    interrogation policy, 30
    and Iran, 128
    Gaza Strip, 29, 35, 44, 49, 51, 52,
        53, 77, 81, 147
    and Hamas, 59
    Military Court, 111
    homeland security, 161-162
    General Security Service. *See*
        General Security Service
        (GSS)
    and PLO, 53

suicide bombings in, 16, 35, 36,
53, 61, 127, 147
West Bank, 29, 35, 52, 75, 116,
139, 143, 147

Jackson, U.S. Senator Henry, 20
Janoff-Bulman, Ronnie, 37
Japanese in U.S. in World War II
internment, 98
Jihad, 34, 43-44, 59
defined, 43
Jongman, Albert, 7
Judicial review, 103
Barak's theory of, 93-94
United States, 98

Kaczynski, Theodore, 16
Kfar Kassem, 68, 75, 76
Khan, Mohammed Sidique, 57
Kovach, Bill, 140
Kurdistan Workers' Party, 48

Lacquer, W., 31
Leahy, Sen. Patrick, 95
Legitimate targets
soldier's determination, 74-77
Liberation Tigers of Tamil Eelam,
32, 33, 48
Lieberman, Trudy, 142
Lindsay, Germaine, 57
London subway bombings, 54, 55,
56-57, 58

Madrid train bombings (2005), 11,
54, 55, 56, 57, 58, 139
Marder, Murrey, 140
McCormack, Professor Wayne,
157
McVeigh, Timothy, 32
and Michigan Militia, 33
Media. *See also* Terrorism
Beslan School attack, 149-150
effect on potential recruits, 146

Munich Olympic Games attack,
137
new vision of media
responsibility, 140-142
Military commissions (U.S.)
combatant status reviews,
113
establishment of, 95
Military Commissions Act (2006,
U.S.)
and *Boumediene v. Bush*, 98
and *Hamdan v. Rumsfeld*, 97,
113
rights denied by, 105
Mohammed, Khalid Sheikh, 117
Mukaskey, Attorney General-
nominee Michael, 105, 112,
113
Mullen, Michael, 94

National security vs. civil and
political rights, 92. *See also*
Individual rights vs. national
security
9/11 Commission Report
on accountability, 162-163
criticism of journalists, 140
and U.S. PATRIOT Act, 97
Non-state actors, 47, 123-125, 169

Open fire orders, 79-89
Operational counterterrorism. *See*
Counterterrorism

Pakistan, 44, 52, 146
Palestine Liberation Organization
(PLO), 15, 17, 127
attack on Israeli Olympic team,
172
compared to Hamas, 53
establishment of, 53
goal, 48
and Soviet Union, 54, 127
Pape, Robert, 33

PATRIOT Act (U.S.)
  business records provision, 57
  definition of terrorist acts
      by, 16
  passage of, 97
Pearl, Daniel, 117, 139, 146, 147
Post, Jerrold, 38
Postman, Neil, 140
Presidential Order (November
      2001), 95
Psychology. *See* Terrorism
Putin, Vladimir
  on Beslan attack, 149

Rabin, Yitzhak, 15, 42
Red Army, 32
Red Brigade, 32
Rehnquist, William H.
  on judicial activism in armed
      conflict, 91, 98
Religion. *See* Terrorism
Rendition to torture, 95
Rice, Secretary of State
      Condoleezza, 139
Rosenstiel, Tom, 140
Russia, 40, 149
  on torture, 11

Saudi Arabia, 49
  terrorist bombing of U.S. military
      in, 54
Schmid, Alex, 7, 9
Security Council Resolutions 1368
      and 1373, 169
Self-defense
  active, 78
  Bush Doctrine, 126
  new vision of, 168-170
  principles
    Caroline doctrine, 169
    Article 51, 169
    UN Resolutions 1368 and 1373,
      169
  and state sponsors, 129
  when to act, 171-173

September 11, 2001 attacks on
      United States, 55
  U.S. responses to, 60
    Authorization of Use of Military
      Force (AUMF), 91-92, 97
    Bush Doctrine, 126
    Military commissions (U.S.), 95
    PATRIOT Act (U.S.), 97
Serrin, W., 141
Sharif, Bassam Abu, 17
Shining Path, 32, 132
Spain
  response to train bombing, 58, 59
Speckhard, Anne, 37
State Department, 109
  definition of terrorism, 11
State sponsors of terror
  designated by U.S., 128
"Strategic corporal," 86. *See also*
      Targeted killing
Strug, Kerri, 116
Sudan, U.S. attacks on, 71
Suicide bombings. *See* Bombings
Supreme Court, U.S., 99, 103
  on detainee rights, 98
  on military commissions, 113
  on rights of suspected terrorists,
      71
Syria, 40
  and Hamas, 124-129

Taliban, 52
  as government of Afghanistan,
      127
Tamil Tigers. *See* Liberation Tigers
      of Tamil Eelam
Targeted killing, 81-87
  alternative means to neutralize
      threat, 87-88
  experience of unit, 86
  soldier's conduct and training,
      84-85
  target behavior, 83-84
Terrorism
  causes of, 15-17
  defined, 7-11, 14

Australia, 9
China, 9
Germany, 10
India, 10
Israel, 10
Japan, 10
Russia, 11
Spain, 11
United Kingdom, 11
U.S., 11
financiers of, 18-20
ideology as motivation, 15, 33,
        40-45
importance of defining, 21-26
levels of support for, 16
and media, 137-148
motivations of, 29-34
psychology as motivation, 36-39
religion as motivation, 33-34
Ticking time bomb theory, 107
TJAGs. *See* Checks and balances
Torture. *See also* Interrogation of
        terrorism suspects
American Psychological
        Association on, 108
Army Field Manual on, 109
defined
        18 U.S.C. §2340, 115
        Convention Against Torture
                (CAT), 115
        International Covenant on
                Civil and Political Rights, 115
European Court of Human
        Rights, 108
rendition to, 95

United Kingdom
homeland security, 162
United Nations. *See also* Security
        Council Resolutions 1368
        and 1373
Charter, 40
CAT (Convention Against
        Torture), 95, 106, 115

United States. *See also* Bush
        Administation
al Qaeda and. *See* September 11,
        2001 attacks on United States
bomb targets outside of
        U.S., 54
Bush Doctrine, 126
definition of terrorism, 11
detainees. *See* Dentention;
        Guantanamo Bay detainees
intelligence gathering
        Foreign Intelligence
                Surveillance Act. *See* Foreign
                Intelligence Surveillance Act
                (FISA)
interrogation of terrorists. *See*
        Interrogation of terrorism
        suspects
judicial review and role of
        Supreme Court, 103
and media, 139-142
military commissions. *See*
        Military commissions (U.S.)
USA PATRIOT Act. *See* PATRIOT Act
        (U.S.)
USS Cole, 141

Weimann, Gabriel, 144
Weapons of mass destruction
        (WMDs), 158
West Bank. *See* Israel
World Trade Center attack (1993),
        54
World Trade Center attack (2001).
        See September 11, 2001
        attacks on United States

Yoo, Professor John, 94

Zapatero, Prime Minister Jose Luis
        Rodriguez, 59
Zemin, President Jiang, 9